THE UNIVERSITY OF
WINCHESTER

Martial Rose Library
Tel: 01962 827306

1 4 DEC 2012

2 1 JAN 2013

To be returned on or before the day marked above, subject to recall.

V
a
Ca

WITHDRAWN FROM
THE LIBRARY
UNIVERSITY OF
WINCHESTER

KA 0336717 7

Post-qualifying Social Work Practice – titles in the series

Critical Thinking for Social Work	ISBN 10: 1 84445 049 X
	ISBN 13: 978 1 84445 049 7
The Approved Social Worker's Guide to Mental Health Law	ISBN 10: 1 84445 062 7
	ISBN 13: 978 1 84445 062 6

To order, please contact our distributor: BEBC Distribution, Albion Close, Parkstone, Poole, BH12 3LL. Telephone: 0845 230 9000, email: learningmatters@bebc.co.uk. You can also find more information on each of these titles and our other learning resources at www.learningmatters.co.uk.

Vulnerable Adults and Community Care

EDITED BY

KEITH BROWN

Series Editor: Keith Brown

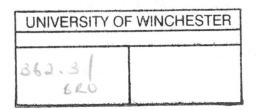

UNIVERSITY OF WINCHESTER

362.3
BRO

First published in 2006 by Learning Matters Ltd

All rights reserved. No part of this publication may be reproduced, stored in a
retrieval system, or transmitted in any form by any means, electronic, mechanical,
photocopying, recording, or otherwise, without prior permission in writing from
Learning Matters.

Copyright Keith Brown

British Library Cataloguing in Publication Data
A CIP record for this book is available from the British Library.

ISBN-10: 1 84445 061 9
ISBN-13: 978 1 84445 061 9

Cover and text design by Code 5 Design Associates Ltd
Project management by Deer Park Productions
Typeset by Pantek Arts Ltd, Maidstone, Kent
Printed and bound in Great Britain by Bell & Bain Ltd, Glasgow

Learning Matters Ltd
33 Southernhay East
Exeter EX1 1NX
Tel: 01392 215560
Email: info@learningmatters.co.uk
www.learningmatters.co.uk

Contents

v

About the authors

Keith Brown

Keith Brown holds professional qualifications in nursing, social work, and teaching and academic qualifications in nursing, social work and management. He has worked in education and training for more than 15 years, working for universities and council social work departments. Currently, Keith is the Head of the Centre for Post Qualifying Social Work at Bournemouth University. The centre was recently recognised with the National Prize at the 2005 National Training Awards and, at the same ceremony, Keith was awarded the Linda Ammon Memorial Prize sponsored by the Department for Education and Skills, given to the person who has made the greatest contribution to education and training in the UK. Keith regularly speaks at national and international conferences. He has also published in national and international journals.

Lee-Ann Fenge

Prior to joining Bournemouth University as a lecturer in 1995, Lee-Ann worked in a number of settings in adult Social Services in both Dorset and London. Her particular interests are in practice with older people, and she is currently engaged in a three-year participative Active Research project with Help and Care. This is working with older lesbians and gay men and supporting them to undertake research on the needs and aspirations of these groups in Dorset. Lee-Ann has also developed and taught a research programme for older people in Community Survey Research – funded by Older and Bolder, September 2004.

Lee-Ann is Head of Widening Participation activity within IHCS and developed a FD Health and Social Care as part of a funded national pilot project for the HNHSU in 2004. Lee-Ann also helped to develop a BA (Hons) Vulnerable Adults/Community Care degree and is currently registered on the Doctor of Professional Practice programme at Bournemouth University. The area of research focused on the experience of students and staff on foundation degrees and work-based learning.

Jason Marshall

Jason completed his Diploma in Social Work in 1999 at Brunel University and added a further year to complete a Degree in Applied Social Studies. Since then he has been working for Social Services in Worcestershire, primarily with adults with acquired brain injury. Jason completed the PQ award in 2006 and it has inspired him to look to a teaching role for himself in the future.

Eileen Qubain

Eileen began her career as a residential social worker, and after training in Cardiff, worked as a hospital social worker for nine years. Eileen now works in a team for older people and feels privileged to work alongside people in crisis. She also feels fortunate to have wonderful colleagues to work with.

Jonathan Monk

Jonathan has worked in social care for over 12 years and has been a qualified social worker since 2000. He joined Worcestershire County Council as a social worker in 2001, working in adult disability services, and was seconded to the post of Direct Payments Development Officer in 2004, to improve access to Direct Payments and promote self-directed care arrangements within mainstream social care services. His work has included extending the scope and uses of Direct Payments; improving training in Direct Payments to enhance knowledge, skills and confidence in Direct Payments; and the development of support services to assist people to use Direct Payments. A central aspect of this work has been involving service users and carers in the development and delivery of Direct Payments within the county. Jonathan sees Direct Payments as a key mechanism for supporting people to improve their quality of life by being fully involved in decision-making and having choice in how their care arrangements are provided.

Chris Willetts

Chris is a Senior Lecturer in Learning Disabilities at Bournemouth University where he is involved in pre and post–qualifying education for social workers, and other health and social care professionals. He also has a range of relevant experience, working with children and adults with a learning disability in a range of care settings.

Marilyn Essex

Marilyn works as a lecturer and Pathway Leader for the Pre Registration Learning Disability Nursing Programme at Bournemouth University. She is also qualified in Adult Nursing with an interest in health promotion and the health of people with learning disabilities. She has experience of working in learning disability services abroad.

Sheeran Zsigo

Sheeran has worked for over 20 years in the field of learning disabilities within various settings, special schools, residential and day care and following social work training, as a care manager in a local authority community learning disabilities team. She is now employed as a lecturer in learning disabilities at Bournemouth University.

Andy Philpott

Andy Philpott is Head of Practice Education, Bournemouth University. After many years working with people with learning disabilities in residential services, he is currently engaged in the education of students who themselves wish to carry on the work with learning disabled people.

Joanna Assey

Joanna is Senior Clinical Nurse Specialist working in the Learning Disability Services of Dorset Healthcare NHS Trust and also is a visiting lecturer at Bournemouth University.

Linda Naylor

Linda Naylor is an independent trainer delivering mainly child and adult protection training for a variety of organisations. She worked as a social worker for 16 years, then as a local authority training officer specialising in adult protection. She was a senior lecturer at Bournemouth University before becoming self-employed. Her training and consultancy in adult protection means she has an overview of the development of this key area of work across the south of England.

Foreword to the Post-qualifying Social Work Practice series

All the texts in the Post-qualifying Social Work Practice series have been written by people with a passion for excellence in social work practice. They are primarily written for social workers who are undertaking post-qualifying social work awards, but will also be useful to any social worker who wants to consider up to date social work practice issues.

The books in the series are also of value to social work students as they are written to inform, inspire and develop social work practice.

All the authors have a connection with the Centre for Post Qualifying Social Work, and as a Centre we are all committed to raising the profile of the social work profession. As a Centre we trust you find this text of real value to your social work practice, and that this in turn has a real impact on the service that users and carers receive.

Keith Brown
Series Editor
Centre for Post Qualifying Social Work

Introduction

This text has primarily been written to support candidates who wish to undertake a post-qualifying social work award, in the field of community care and working with vulnerable adults. It is designed to support students studying for the new post-qualifying specialist award in adult services.

It is written as a series of self-contained chapters to support learning and development by colleagues and ex-students from within the Centre for Post Qualifying Social Work at Bournemouth University. Their combined experience and expertise is considerable and clear for all to see from their contributions.

The self-contained chapters are written in such a way as to help candidates on post-qualifying social work awards think about how they might structure their own work with regards to demonstrating their competence to practice. Given the breadth of experience of the writers, the text is also extremely valuable to current practitioners of social work with adults as a means to reflect on contemporary practice issues.

Keith Brown
Head of the Centre for Post Qualifying Social Work

This book will help you to meet the following Occupational Standards for Social Work:

Key Role 1: unit 3:	Assess need and options to recommend a course of action
Key Role 2: unit 5:	Interact with individuals, families, carers, groups and communities to achieve change and development and to improve life opportunities
Key Role 2: unit 7:	Support the development of networks to meet assessed needs and planned outcomes
Key Role 2: unit 8:	Work with groups to promote individual growth, development and independence
Key Role 4: unit 12:	Assess and manage risks to individuals, families, carers, groups and communities
Key Role 5: unit 14:	Manage and be accountable for yourself
Key Role 5: unit 15:	Contribute to the management of resources and services
Key Role 5: unit 17:	Work within multi-disciplinary and multi-organisational teams, networks and systems
Key Role 6: unit 18:	Research, analyse, evaluate and use current knowledge of best social work practice
Key Role 6: unit 19:	Work within agreed standards of social work practice and ensure own professional development
Key Role 6: unit 20:	Manage complex ethical issues, dilemmas and conflicts
Key Role 6: unit 21:	Contribute to the promotion of best social work practice

If you are a registered social worker, this book will assist you to evidence post-registration training and learning. It relates to the national post-qualifying framework for social work education and training, especially the national criteria at the specialist level, in particular:

(i)   Meet the relevant academic standards associated with social work at this level.

(iv) Draw on knowledge and understanding of service users' and carers' issues to actively contribute to strategies and practice which promote service users' and carers' rights and participation in line with the goals of choice, independence and empowerment.

(v)   Use reflection and critical analysis to continuously develop and improve their specialist practice, including their practice in inter-professional and inter-agency contexts, drawing systematically, accurately and appropriately on theories, models and relevant up-to-date research.

(vi) Extend initial competence so as to develop in-depth competence in the context of one area of specialist practice to agreed national specialist standards, drawing on knowledge and experience of the range of settings and service systems that impact on the lives of service users.

(vii) Work effectively in a context of risk, uncertainty, conflict and contradiction.

(x)   Effectively manage own work and demonstrate a capacity to plan for and respond to change in organisational, inter-organisational and team contexts.

Chapter 1
Welfare policy: context of community care

Keith Brown

INTRODUCTION

This first chapter aims to consider and analyse British welfare policy and its recent developments and its impact on the community care agenda. Although it is in essence a social policy analysis, it is written to provide a clear background to the policy context within which social workers currently deliver community care. The philosophical areas of welfare capitalism and free market thinking are considered in order to give a background to the current situation that social workers find themselves working within.

Social workers as professionals regulated by the General Social Care Council are required to abide by a set of professional standards which at their heart rightly have the needs of service users and carers. Yet the vast majority of social workers work for social work agencies (usually local authority social service departments) which have great budgeting pressures on them.

The central government pressure to keep down the cost of the council tax (Community Charge) is at odds with ever increasing pressure for more and better quality services, particularly for vulnerable adults. Thus councils are forced to prioritise (another word for ration) their service in order to stay within budget and this puts a pressure on the social worker. Here the social worker is under pressure as the resources the client might need may be simply too expensive. Also, there is the strange pressure which says 'please do not be effective in finding new clients who want help as we cannot afford to meet their needs.' In other words, in financial terms, it is better to employ social workers whose skills and abilities are in preventing new clients from wanting, seeking or finding help.

This chapter looks at the background to this dilemma and the developments of Welfare Policy which underpin the delivery of social work in the UK.

Welfare capitalism

Introduction

The aim of this section of the chapter is to provide a general sketch of a welfare perspective usually referred to as 'welfare capitalism'. (It has also been called 'collectivism', 'the post-war consensus', 'Butskellism' (Butler/Gatskill) and the 'Keynesian welfare state').

Welfare capitalism dominated British governments' economic and welfare conceptions in the post-war years between 1945 and 1977. In terms of other societies, welfare capitalism forms an important ideological base for the economics and politics of: Australia, Austria, Canada, Finland and Sweden, and looks to be the conception of capitalism that many of the Eastern European countries (e.g. Russia, the Baltic States, Poland, Hungary and Slovakia) are taking as their models of future provision.

Basic characteristics

Welfare capitalism is a combination of:

- Keynesian values and economic instruments concerning the organisation, administration and regulation of the economy, and

- a conception of welfare and welfare provision that uses universal principles and (predominantly) state-welfare programmes, and which seeks to ensure that all citizens have the resources needed to participate in the social (and economic) life of society.

Welfare capitalism advocates:

- **a mixed economy**, that is, an economy with both a public sector (i.e. owned and/or regulated industries and services) and a substantial private sector;

- **a government committed to Keynesian economics**, committed, that is, to using the fiscal and monetary controls as a way of regulating the economy;

- **state-financed and state-provided welfare**; and

- **a free trade union movement** that can pursue its objectives in a way that is compatible with the survival of a mixed economy and a Keynesian state.

The general economic goal of welfare capitalism is full employment. This, however, is not an end in itself; it operates in the service of a higher political goal that, for the moment, we can summarise as 'social justice'. Keynesian economic measures provide the state with the means of managing the economy. Managing the economy in a way that reduces instability, minimises unemployment and eliminates poverty, is seen as an important step along the road to social justice. The operations of the welfare state are regarded as treading a similar political path. They are designed to reduce the impact of unemployment where it exists, eliminate the extremes of poverty and generate a better quality of life.

They do so through:

- the provision of payments for the old, the sick, the disabled and the unemployed, and

- the supply of basic services – such as health, social services and education – to all of society's members regardless of their income, gender, class or ethnicity.

The support for welfare capitalism

Welfare capitalism's adherents range from reluctant supporters (academic conservatives like Beveridge and Keynes, and Conservative Party politicians such as Macmillan, Butler and Heath,) through to positive advocates (academic Fabian socialists like T.H. Marshall, Titmuss, Townsend and Plant, and Labour Party politicians such as Atlee, Bevan, Crosland and Gaitskell).

The reluctant nature of conservative (and Conservative) support derives from the uneasy relation between state intervention in the economy (which both groups attempt to limit) and their concern to enhance the possibility of greater individual liberty. Basically, state intervention is seen to restrict individual liberty. But they maintain better some compromise between individual freedom and state intervention than the vagaries of the free market. The spectre haunting conservatives (and Conservative adherents) is mass unemployment and the more specific instance of the degradation and poverty that beset Britain, Europe and America in the economic depression of the 1930s. Keynesian forms of economic intervention and the corresponding welfare state are seen to offer a safety net, inhibiting a repetition of such events (this indeed is what conservatives mean by 'social justice').

Socialist support for welfare capitalism operates from different grounds. It is a fundamental belief of Fabians that economic production and distribution should be subjected to governmental regulation in the pursuit of the higher political and moral goals of liberty and equality (the Fabian conception of 'social justice'). Economic regulation is an essential means of promoting social justice, or enhancing individual self-development and fostering a sense of community. The rationale for such regulation is provided through a contrast with free-market capitalism, welfare capitalism's recognised alternative:

> *the free market is defective because the distribution of goods and services/income and wealth that occurs through the operation of the market does not secure social justice...Given the inevitably random element in market outcomes, those whose needs are not met by the market have a defensible moral claim on the resources of those who are successful in the market. Hence, left to its own devices, the market causes injustice, an injustice which can only be rectified either by state intervention in the market...or by the state providing an alternative to markets via welfare provision.*

> (Raymond Plant, in Le Grand J. and Estrin S. eds, 1990, p54)

In what follows, the major features of welfare capitalism are discussed through the arguments and proposals of its socialist advocates – the Fabians. After sketching the political values of the position, there will be a focus on its economics and its view of welfare policy and provision.

The political values of welfare capitalism[1]

The central values

Because of the importance they attach to the role of ideas and ideals in history, Fabians have a lot to say about the kind of social values which they consider essential to socialism. They stress three central values – equality, freedom and fellowship – and two derivative values – democratic participation which is the child of equality and freedom, and humanitarianism *which is the offspring of equality and fellowship...these five (values) make up the basic value-mix of British democratic socialism.*

(George and Wilding, 1985, 69–70)

By *equality* Fabians mean:

...more than a meritocratic society of equal opportunities... more than a simple... redistribution of income. We (want) a wider social equality embracing also the distribution of property, the educational system, social-class relationships, power and privilege in industry – indeed, all that (is) enshrined in the age-old dream of a more 'classless society'.

(Crosland,1974, p40)

Equality is an instrumental value, in other words, it is the consequences that are derived from implementing egalitarian policies that are important, not the notion per se. When such policies are successful, the outcomes are not simply greater equality but greater social integration, increased economic efficiency, better opportunities for self-realisation and greater freedom.

Greater *freedom* is valued in a non-instrumental way, if not as *the* major value of welfare capitalism. We might best describe what Fabians mean by freedom through the use of Berlin's wall.

Berlin describes two distinct kinds of freedom, positive freedom and negative freedom. By negative freedom, he means the absence of coercion:

Coercion implies the deliberate interference of other human beings within the area in which I could otherwise act. You lack political liberty or freedom only if you are prevented from attaining a goal by human beings. Mere incapacity to attain a goal is not lack of freedom.

(Berlin, 1969, p122)

By positive freedom he means:

...the wish on the part of the individual to be his own master. I wish my life and decisions to depend on myself, not on external forces of whatever kind.

(ibid, p131)

---

1 This section draws on chapter 4 of George and Wilding's text *Ideology and Social Welfare*, The Fabian Socialists' well known essay *Two Concepts of Liberty*.

Fabians have little time for 'negative freedom' mainly because it ignores what they regard as important barriers to liberty. Poverty, illiteracy and unemployment are examples of such barriers. They would be ignored by negative liberty because there is no implication of 'deliberate interference'. The Fabian philosopher Raymond Plant makes the point in this way:

> *The limitations on individual freedom are not just those imposed deliberately by intentional actions of others...(there are) also those limitations which are imposed by natural differences of birth and genetic inheritance, together with those which are the result of human action, whether deliberate or not, in the field of family background, economic resources, welfare and education.*

(Plant, 1984, p6)

For Fabians, the preferred conception of freedom is what Berlin terms 'positive freedom'. Positive freedom is a liberty that allows:

> *...me to live a meaningful life, to live it in my own way, shaped by my own values and purposes. This is a noble idea, and one which goes to the heart of what it is for a purposive creature to live a meaningful life.*

(Plant, ibid p6)

Fabians combine this notion of liberty with their instrumental conception of egalitarianism. Egalitarian policies should be designed to maximise individual freedom. Policies that counter poverty, racism, sexism, unemployment, illiteracy, and the social inequalities of having physical and mental disabilities ought to be designed to create 'equality of value' – equal dignity. By such means they should enhance individual liberty.

Closely linked with this conception of individual freedom (and therefore equality) is the Fabian notion of 'fellowship'. By *fellowship* they mean:

> *co-operation rather than competition...the good of the community rather than the wants of the individual...altruism rather than selfishness.*

(George and Wilding, op cit p74)

Democratic participation and *humanitarianism* complement the primary political values. Democratic participation enhances the Fabian belief in political and economic freedom. What it basically involves is the recognition that democracy should exist in all aspects of people's lives – in their work situations and in their local communities. Humanitarianism, in Fabian terms, involves the belief that there should be minimum standards of living and, further, that these minimum standards must be capable of alleviating the variety of forms of social stress to which people become subject. The clear corollary to this concerns the significance and level of welfare provision and the continued commitment to its maintenance.

These five values are often interwoven by Fabians through the general notions of *citizenship* and *social justice*. The state is the guarantor of equal liberty. It has to be concerned not only with political and civil liberties but also with the resources, opportunities, powers and rights which people need if they are to act as citizens. Welfare policies, it is maintained, should seek to be socially just; the just (egalitarian) distribution of social and economic resources enables those who are impoverished to exercise the freedom that the better placed have by virtue of income and education.

Free-market capitalism – the Conservative years 1979–1997

Free-market conceptions of society, the economy and politics dominated nineteenth century political economy. In the twentieth century it:

> *lapsed into academic and political obscurity – particularly between 1940 and 1970. The (economic) recession which overtook many of the advanced industrial countries from the early 1970s however, encouraged a resurgence of (free-market) thinking. Its advocates – (such as Hayek) – gained a new eminence and influence.*

> (George and Wilding,1985, p19)

In the 1940s, 1950s and 1960s then, it was possible to regard free-market thinking as a system of thought belonging to another age. By the mid to late 1970s, however, such a viewpoint was no longer possible. Under Margaret Thatcher's leadership, initially in opposition and then in government, the Conservative Party revived and utilised free-market thinking as the basis of its economic, political and welfare policies. Quite why it developed with this change of leadership is a matter of speculation, after all, Enoch Powell was arguing a very similar kind of free-market thinking in the 1960s and it met with scant attention from those same politicians (Margaret Thatcher and Keith Joseph among them) who have openly embraced these views since the 1970s. Gamble offers the following explanation:

> *What made possible the rise (of free-market thinking) in the 1970s was the widespread perception in the (Conservative) Party that the Heath government had been a failure, and that Britain was becoming ungovernable. This coincided with the onset of world recession and increasing alarm about the implications of Britain's continuing relative decline. The climate of failure and indecision that clung to British governments in the 1960s and 1970s gave the political opportunity for a sharp break with both the rhetoric and practice of post-war (Keynesian) economics.*

> (Gamble, cited in Levitas, 1986, p49)

For Gamble then, it was less the intrinsic merits of free-market thinking than the perceived failure of Keynesianism that led the Conservatives under Margaret Thatcher's leadership to seek an alternative theoretical/philosophical terrain to that occupied by all governments since the Second World War.

A characterisation of the theoretical elements of Conservative free-market thinking

There are three elements to the free-market thinking propounded by Conservatives since the mid-1970s:

- libertarianism;

- the doctrine of economic individualism;

- the Austrian school's conception of liberal political economy.

Libertarianism

One of the best-known statements of this position is made by Robert Nozick. (See, for example, his Anarchy, State and Utopia*). He argues that the minimal state, the state which protects the lives and property of its citizens, can be justified, but nothing beyond the minimal state. Any use of the state's coercive powers beyond this minimum infringes individual rights. Libertarianism carries hostility to government to its furthest extreme. Its concept of the economy is constructed on the basis of the absolute character of the property rights of the individual.*

(Gamble, ibid, p30)

In many ways, libertarianism is the least significant of these elements. It occasionally provides both Ministers and Conservative backbenchers with rhetoric – generally in their pronouncements of opposition to the quantity and cost of (central and local) government services – but it provides little more. Why? Because, as Gamble points out, the logical extension of the libertarian belief in the rights of individuals to own property, to create markets and to buy and sell whatever is wished without restriction, is also an effective justification for *free markets in heroin and pornography as well as (opposition to) controls on immigration.* This would be anathema to current Conservatism and conflicts sharply with its commitment to an economic individualism (and its accompanying morality).

The doctrine of economic individualism

This is traditional laissez-faire (i.e. free-market) economics which assumes without question that markets are beneficial and governments harmful, and that individual freedom and government exist in inverse ratio to each other. The best-ordered economy is therefore one in which scope for individual choice is greatest and scope for government responsibility smallest. The level of taxation is the most important measure of this. The more taxed citizens are, the less free (they are).

(Gamble, ibid, p30)

The doctrine of economic individualism with its commitment to market production and distribution, and its belief in economic choice is of some importance to current Conservatives and has led to the rejuvenation of ideas of self-help, competition and personal responsibility. Although it is of much greater significance than libertarianism, it is nonetheless of lesser importance than the third element – the Austrian school of economics.

The Austrian school of economics

The approach of the Austrian school of economics stems from the work of Carl Menger, but it is the specific work of one of Menger's students, Friedrich Hayek, which has been a major influence on British Conservatives' free-market thinking. The distinctive features of the school's approach are not simply its economics (in which it refused to accept the methodology of neo-classical positive economics or to focus attention on equilibrium theory), but its citing of economic issues within the wider context of political economy and, therein, its intractable opposition to socialist political economy.

A Caveat

There needs to be care regarding language at this point. To speak of a source of ideas being 'a major influence' or 'having an impact' is not to suggest that the Conservative government's free-market thinking can be reduced to Hayekian first principles. Hayek's views did not determine or structure government policy in the previous Conservative government. They do not possess the status of edicts so much as guidelines for a free-market economy. They have been used by Margaret Thatcher and John Major in the development of economic, trade union and welfare legislation and policy.

Hayek's conception of political economy can be organised around three central notions:

- freedom;

- the market economy;

- his opposition to welfare capitalism.

Freedom

Hayek makes it very clear that the political conception which is of paramount importance is the notion of freedom or liberty. In *The Constitution of Liberty*, Hayek defines freedom as the absence of coercion.

> *We are concerned in this book with that condition (of people) in which coercion of some by others is reduced as much as is possible in society. This state we shall describe throughout as a state of liberty or freedom. The task of a policy of freedom must therefore be to minimise coercion or its harmful effects, even if it cannot eliminate it completely.*

> (Hayek, 1960, pp11–12)

Note here:

- The undivided nature of this conception of freedom, i.e. Hayek is not discussing particular freedoms or an aggregate of particular freedoms, he is saying that freedom is no more and no less than the absence of coercion.

- Freedom's inverse relation with coercion: to maximise freedom we must minimise coercion.

- That coercion concerns those situations in which people are forced to serve the interests of others, rather than pursue their own interests. It concerns the *intentional* actions of human agents.

Hayek believes that coercion by individuals is something that can be drastically reduced if one social agency, the state, is able to punish individuals who infringe laws governing individual exchange. But the problem then becomes one of how to reduce the coercion of the state itself. Hayek's answer is the construction of a private sphere free from public intervention. Such a sphere can only come into existence if there are certain activities and rights that are protected and cannot be infringed by government. This requires that:

- the government as well as individuals are bound by laws and that decisions of Ministers, civil servants or other government agents can be subject to legal appeal and reversal in the courts;

- and the government recognises the limits to its power through a conception of non-coercive government activity.

Such a conception, of course, conflicts with the idea of 'popular sovereignty' because it implies that there are laws that should be beyond the power of a government to alter. The doctrine of popular sovereignty would suggest that a government elected by the people has the right to overturn and redesign all laws.

Hayek's concern here is to preserve freedom by limiting the power of a legislative assembly, no matter how democratically constituted it is. He is not anti-democracy as such; indeed he sees it as the least harmful of governmental forms. For him, its benefits include that it:

- provides a peaceful way of resolving conflicts;

- provides the best way of educating people about public affairs;

- can act as a safeguard for individual liberty.

Nonetheless, democracy is flawed. In particular, it threatens freedom by creating the possibility of unlimited power for majority governments that could lead them into abuses involving increased state intervention.

The market economy

Defining freedom as he does, and expressing a degree of distrust in democracy as a result, leads Hayek to certain views of economic policy. In particular, he draws a simple equation between freedom and the market economy. The market is to be the sphere of free, voluntary, individual behaviour regulated by law and protected from the coercion practised either by individuals or the state. It is an economy in which:

- economic power is decentralised;

- the division of labour is coordinated by the market;

- income is distributed through the free operation of market forces;

- the role of government is confined to the enforcement of those general rules, for example on contract and property that define the market order and make market relations possible. It needs to be vigilant and strong to enforce competition and outlaw private coercive power. But it has no role or justification in seeking to intervene directly in the decisions individuals take in the market.

Main suppositions

1. Hayek is committed to individualism, in other words, he does not accept that society possesses 'structures' (such as social classes) influencing the activities of people. Society is no more than an abstraction of the aggregate of individual activities. But what is it that maintains societal organisation? As you might guess from the preceding paragraphs, the answer is the role of law. Laws are necessary for both the operation of the market and the existence of individual liberty. They specify the grounds and conditions under which government would use its powers to protect individual economic and political liberty.

2. Market forces constitute the best mechanism for the production and allocation of goods and services in society.

3. Where there is need for some state provision of services, the extent of such public provision should be carefully specified and deliberately minimised.

4. Given that freedom is market freedom, maximising market processes will also maximise political and economic freedom.

5. Markets work not on altruism but on individual self-interest. Competition is the 'keyword'; individuals compete in terms of both conflicting and common interests.

6. The individual pursuit of self-interest generates 'spontaneous co-operative activity', voluntary exchanges of goods and services. And since it is voluntary, exchange will only take place if both parties feel that they will benefit from it.

7. Free markets are more successful than planning in coping with uncertainty, because the knowledge available to planning authorities is nowhere near as great as the knowledge dispersed in a market among all its agents. Planning authorities would have no means of assessing whether their planning decisions were efficient or not, since prices would no longer be set by the forces of supply and demand (and thus by the competition between individual producers and consumers).

Hayek's opposition to welfare capitalism

Hayek's opposition to welfare capitalism is primarily based on an analysis in which his own views (of freedom and the market) are used as measures of Fabian proposals.

On planning and the economy: planning in any form, whether in the older style East European Communist planned economy or in the Keynesian conception of a managed economy, is regarded as an unnecessary and unwarranted intrusion that leads to a reduction of liberty. For Hayek, the institutional form of a market economy is not a political option; it is the mark of modern civilisation. Therefore it cannot be changed by political decree without threatening civilisation. This is why ideas of planning come in for such strong criticism. Planning is an atavistic move, a throwback to a more primitive way of life. It ignores all the complexities of the modern economic world that generated economic progress.

Of the managed economy: capitalism, Hayek maintains, is about the creation of wealth by individuals taking risks in the market and launching new enterprises. Real aggregate demand in the economy, he argues, is an effect of production not policy. Hence governments are powerless to affect real aggregate demand (in the way Keynesians suggest) through policies of taking and spending. What governments should be doing instead is encouraging entrepreneurial activities and the creation of wealth by reducing taxation.

All alternatives to markets are flawed: a great deal of effort has been devoted by the Austrian school (and Hayek in particular) to demonstrating that the basic ideas of socialism contain logical flaws, and further, that socialism cannot provide a rational means of economic organisation. Only an economic system based on private ownership can achieve an *efficient* allocation of resources and the greatest possible increase in wealth and productivity.

On equality: Hayek maintains that equality and freedom are usually at odds; to pursue equality is usually to suppress freedom. Equality generally demands state intervention and state intervention involves coercion. Given the paramount importance of freedom, general egalitarian policies must be abandoned.

In commenting on specific egalitarian policies (such as the redistribution of income through progressive taxation), Hayek suggests that they:

● discourage the creation of wealth;

● inhibit efficiency and productivity.

The only exceptions to his general stance on equality concerns are those equalities that are seen to enhance freedom, namely:

● civil and political liberties like equality before the law and electoral rights;

● equality of opportunity.

The rejection of social justice: social justice, Hayek maintains, is not something that should feature in discussions of political economy. There is nothing just or unjust about market outcomes. What matters, for Hayek, is not the market's distribution of rewards but the concept of 'market order', based on general rules which guarantee everyone maximum opportunities. Actual distribution is a lottery – the chance of material inheritance and the manner in which opportunities arise. He defends this lottery approach to the market's distribution of rewards by maintaining that no better system can be devised. There are no principles of justice that permit a central authority to redistribute income more fairly. Redistribution undertaken by the state is as arbitrary as the system of rewards that it is trying to replace, and by legitimising intervention in the economy it is being undertaken at the expense of freedom.

The attack on trade unions: according to Hayek, trades unions have a legitimate role in society as voluntary associations, but their role should be strictly limited. In large scale organisations, collective agreements on rules governing conditions of work, promotions and pay differentials may assist the smooth running of business. He also recognises the value of trades unions functioning as friendly societies insuring their members against sickness and unemployment. Unions become a problem and a threat to freedom, once allowed to develop beyond these functions:

> *Public policy concerning labour unions has, in little more than a century, moved from one extreme to the other. From a state in which little the unions could do was legal if they were not prohibited altogether, we have now reached a state where they have become uniquely privileged institutions to which the general rules of law do not apply. They have become the only important instance in which governments signally fail in their prime function – the prevention of coercion and violence.*

(Hayek, 1960, p267)

Hayek claims the following.

● Unions have become private monopolies, able to pursue their objectives only by the coercion of some of their members or other workers;

- Unions *cannot in the long-run increase real wages for all wishing to work, above the level that would establish itself in a free market* (Hayek, ibid, p270). Given this is so, he maintains that it therefore follows that if unions seek to raise wages above this level for some workers, they can only do so by harming others, by lowering their wages or forcing redundancies;

- The existence of national and industrial unions, rather than company or plant unions, causes major damage to the economy. It distorts relative wages, restricts the mobility of labour and deters investment.

For the sake of freedom and the free-functioning of the market order, trades unions must be returned to a status of small-scale (i.e. company or plant-based) voluntary associations that cease from interfering with the manager's right to manage, or pursuing claims for increased wages above market valuations.

The welfare policies of free-market thinking on state welfare

State welfare is considered to supplant the free market with:

- its 'excessive' tax demands;

- and by making itself a near monopoly supplier in many welfare areas.

With its proliferation of services it is seen to undermine the family and individual responsibilities, and, with its system of benefits, to have produced a culture of dependency and irresponsibility.

What do free-market thinkers want in place of state welfare provision?

Ideally... a situation in which the supply (of welfare services) is both competitive and privately owned, and (where) the demand (for services) consists of unsubsidised individual purchases.

(Hudson, 1989, p1546)

Such an ideal is seen to have several advantages over current state welfare:

The advantage of the demand side is that people are able to maximise their individual welfare functions constrained only by their willingness and ability to pay, rather than by governmental budgetary constraint...

On the supply side the advantages arise from competition for customers and profits. This competition allows enterprises to satisfy consumer demand efficiently, by looking for profitable opportunities and seeking innovation.

(Flynn, 1989, p10)

The political values underwriting this welfare mixture should be reasonably clear:

(M)arket mechanisms should be used wherever possible.

(Hudson, 1989 p1546)

Sir Geoffrey Howe makes the point in the following way:

> *Putting markets and competition to work in the nation's interests is not just a policy for industry or local government. It is (also) an approach (for) the apparatus of the welfare state.*

(From a speech in 1983, quoted in Loney, 1986)

- *(C)ompetition should be established between providers, even if this is largely the public sector competing within itself;*
- *(C)onsumers should be allowed to opt out of state provision in order to sharpen competition;*
- *(I)ndividualism and individual choice should take precedence over collective choices and planned provision;*
- *(I)f possible, individuals should manage without help from institutions of any sort, except their own families.*

> *(A)s a party committed to the family and opposed to the all-powerful state, we want people to keep more of what they earn, and to have more freedom of choice about what they do for themselves, their families and others less fortunate.*

(Hudson, ibid, p1546)

The Thatcher/Major-led governments used several instruments in pursuing these values that included:

- reducing public expenditure on statutory welfare services;
- privatising statutory services;
- shifting the expectations and the realities of care of:
  a) the consumers of welfare services;
  b) their carers/families;
  c) welfare practitioners and their managers.

Welfare based on these values will, according to free-market thinkers, create a new agenda for welfare: an agenda that is both more realistic and enables greater efficiency.

Social exclusion and paradoxes for social work

Social work universally appears to have its basis firmly rooted in a welfare capitalist ideology. There is almost universal acceptance that at its heart are notions of equality and freedom. Social workers world-wide attempt to counter discrimination of all kinds. Indeed the Central Council for Education and Training in Social Work (CCETSW) in England state in their Equal Opportunities Policy Statement:

> *Providers of social care and social work education and training and assessment centres will eliminate unfair discrimination and disadvantage in all aspects of their work regulated by the Council.*

(CCETSW, 1996)

However, as we have seen, a free market capitalist system based on Hayek's principles is fundamentally opposed to society influencing the activities of people. It is committed to individualism where the individual is responsible for him/herself. If you pursue equality you will suppress freedom. Therefore given the paramount importance of freedom, general egalitarian policies must be abandoned.

Social work thus has no mandate for working towards creating equality, and the state should not be involved in this activity. Social work is thus reduced to a free market commercial activity responding to individual consumer interests. Indeed, social exclusion will be seen as a positive indication that the market economy is working and is to be expected.

The only exception to this will be specific state run or financed social work of the police type social work within mental health or child protection.

The obvious conclusions for social work are thus at first sight quite depressing. However, perhaps one aspect has been forgotten by the free-market thinkers. It is the capacity for individual people to group together in communities/societies for the greater good of all. Perhaps individuals will look at their neighbours and decide to care for the entire human race; or will greed and the individual remain dominant?

The Third Way

The term 'Third Way' is not a new term and can be traced to Pope Pius XII in the nineteenth century who called for a third way between socialism and capitalism. Bill Clinton used the term in his State of the Union speech:

> *We have moved past the sterile debate between those who say government is the enemy and those who say government is the answer. My fellow Americans, we have found a Third Way.*

Jordan (2000) suggests the term 'Third Way' has been adopted by Tony Blair's New Labour government as a name for its political philosophy and strategy. There has been a lot of debate over what is meant by the term. In a NEXUS hosted on-line discussion in 1998, Stewart Wood (Fellow in Politics, Magdalen College, Oxford) stated that it represented *a form of political product differentiation without really knowing what the product is*.

One way of trying to understand the Third Way is by seeing it as a relationship between the individual and the community, and a redefinition of rights and obligations. It seeks to revive civic culture and utilise the dynamics of markets, but with the public interest in mind.

Clearly there is some debate as to whether this is possible and, as previously mentioned, it could be argued that much of the welfare of the Third Way is directed towards the better off as the marginalised in society do not tend to vote in general elections.

The politics of community and the Third Way

The concept of community notoriously has many meanings, 57 according to Leaper in 1971. We can probably triple that number all these years later. Why the preoccupation to define community? Jordan (2000) argues community has a key role in bringing together the two main moral traditions of individualist and collectivist ideology to create a Third Way morality for government at a macro level, and service provision within health and social care at a micro level.

Individualism

Individualism is biased towards institutions that enable individuals to be responsible for themselves, to be morally autonomous, and to be committed to personal projects and relationships. It sees group ethics and collectivist institutions as intrusive and distorting of individuals' potential. It holds individuals to account for the outcomes of their decisions and choices. It sees justice primarily in terms of the procedures and rules that govern inter-actions, and therefore favours institutions such as markets and adversarial court hearings.

Collectivism

Collectivism is biased towards institutions that promote care, mutuality, solidarity and inter-dependence. It emphasises equality of membership, dignity and decency in all interactions, as factors enabling trust and co-operation. It sees individualistic ethics and morality as pro-moting selfishness and social irresponsibility. It holds individuals responsible for contributing to the common good, and restraining their competitive impulses. It sees jus-tice in terms of the distribution process, as concerned with fair shares of the benefits of co-operation.

Community

What the different meanings imply is that membership of a community involves a degree of reciprocity and co-operation, and mutual obligation and responsibility. In liberal politi-cal thought, a high priority is placed on individual freedom and on protection against interference or coercion by others or the state. Conversely, collectivism invests the state with formidable coercive powers, involving strong restraint of individual liberties and interests, and an authoritarian role in the pursuit of common purposes, what Jordan (2000) describes as an *objective* version of the *good society* (p50).

Therefore, community in a political and policy context is both a system of order and mem-bership, and a way of getting things done; it is both a form of social organisation and a kind of economy. In the latter sense, as a way of producing and distributing goods and services, it is an alternative to markets and state services.

The Third Way focuses on community almost entirely as a system of social control, with members holding each other responsible for orderly conduct and work contributions, and thus providing the 'glue' to bind an inclusive society together (Williams, 1998).

New Labour, the Third Way and the welfare state

New Labour and the Third Way emphasises collaboration rather than competition and decreased reliance on market and quasi market forces, long-term effectiveness rather than short-term efficiency.

These are the key principles for the reform of the welfare state.

- An 'enabling' welfare state that promotes social and economic inclusion.

- The welfare state should address the causes of poverty and promote participation in the labour market.

- Welfare policies should deliver social and economic inclusion and ease the transition from welfare benefits to paid employment.

- A skilled workforce is crucial to national competitive efficiency.

- Rather than a redistribution of wealth and income, the role of the state is to provide citizens with opportunities for education and training, thus enhancing individual life chances.

Commentators have argued that New Labour's focus on paid employment does not deal with inequality. The idea of labour market inclusion uncritically accommodates the wealthy in the 'in work' majority and thus fails to challenge existing distributions of wealth and power. It presents an overly homogenous image of society in which many inequalities exist. The emphasis on paid employment does not recognise unpaid work, such as caring or parenting, as a legitimate contribution to society.

New Labour argue that the New Right's attempt to withdraw the state and promote individualism and markets eroded communal and co-operative values. In contrast, New Labour's welfare programme embodies the idea of citizens, linked together by reciprocal duties and responsibilities, who collaborate with the state in a co-operative enterprise to ensure an economically vibrant country.

They call for greater accountability founded on co-operation and partnership, focusing on managerial techniques that build on partnership and strategic alliances. They also call for decentralisation, flexibility, freedom from bureaucracy, entrepreneurialism and local autonomy.

Welfare revolution: true or false?

In the 60 years since the inception of the welfare state, all aspects of social services have been targets of unprecedented masses of legislation, much of it creating new powers, duties and responsibilities for social services. During the last decades of the twentieth century a second revolution in social policy could be said to have taken place, as many welfare services were reconstituted and privatised, and markets were created for the purchase and delivery of services. Local government was subjected to transformation by complex arrangements involving the public, private and voluntary sectors.

Have any of these changes significantly improved the quality of life of specific groups of individuals? On the whole, those who already have wealth and are higher earners have fared well, however, according to Powell (2001), welfare policies during the twentieth century have left the living conditions of many of the worse off largely unchanged.

Powell goes on to suggest there is evidence that unemployment, inadequate housing, deficient health and community care, low incomes and problems associated with poverty still particularly affect people experiencing physical or learning disabilities, older people,

people with mental health problems, lone parents, those with less earning capacity, children in poor families, and families living in resource starved urban and rural districts where access to welfare services is far from adequate.

The poor are still viewed with a mixture of sympathy and suspicion, depending on the extent to which they are regarded as trying to help themselves. Stereotypes of the homeless beggar, the 'morally' deficient single parent (usually a mother), the 'dangerous' 'mad' person (who fluctuates between mad, bad or sad), the disabled person deemed as a lesser person as they do not meet the 'norm' physically and/or mentally, or the older person 'past it' and invisible to society, are still dominated by prejudices rather than informed realities of their circumstances and the experiences of people themselves.

The focus on the undeniable changes in the welfare services, and how they are organised, managed and delivered, diverts attention from the unchanging realities of being poor, being alone, experiencing health problems, becoming older and living in a society which discriminates against people who are different, whether through class, gender, age, ethnicity, disability, sexuality or any other social division.

New Labour – Third Way – where are we going?

There are a number of key texts which evaluate the impact of New Labour's reforms to the welfare state since 1997, when the Labour party came to power. (See Jordan, 1998; Powell, 2002; Clarke, 2000; Jordan, 2000).

One of the interesting aspects of social policy development has been the emphasis in Welfare to Work. Here the welfare state has been used to encourage people back to work, so that they cease to be a burden on society. One could argue that the reduction that has been seen in unemployment figures is a testimony to the effectiveness of this strategy.

However, as is considered in Chapter 7, this has a consequence in the number of people available to work in informal care and thus it increases the pressure on Community Care.

Another aspect of the welfare policy under New Labour has been the emphasis on targets and tables, in an attempt to increase the quality of care in certain areas. For example there is much attention to the needs of the acute ill health sector and casualty waiting lists, with a host of strategies mentioned elsewhere in this text as to how best to 'improve' this situation. But there is little emphasis on the marginalised groups and Cinderella areas such as learning disabilities. Indeed one could draw the conclusion that the aim of New Labour welfare policy is to move away from free-market principles towards a welfare capitalist system for those services that meet the needs of the middle class voters, whilst providing little new resources to those marginalised within society other than an encouragement to seek employment to reduce the burden on society.

This movement of the value base for the welfare system produces a fundamental dilemma for social work practice if social work sees itself as a profession with a core value to work to promote equality and to attempt to eliminate inequality. The value base of social work thus comes into conflict with the value base of the welfare policy of society.

The various chapters in this book look at and consider this issue. Hopefully they will help you as a social worker to consider your own value base whilst also helping to equip you with a clear basis for your social work practice.

As a final point, we saw at the last general election the ultimate irony of a Conservative opposition leader, Iain Duncan Smith, suggesting that if elected a Conservative government would abolish university tuition fees whilst a current Labour government is proposing to raise the fees (*Times* Editorial, 13 May 2003).

Questions

- Which political party has its roots in the free market and which party has its roots in the welfare state? This confusion is often a major issue when looking at welfare policy and social work delivery in Britain.

- Amid the complexities of social work practice in the twenty first century, how do you perceive yourself as a professional and how does this impact on your practice? What has influenced you most as a professional in practice and why?

Chapter 2

Community care: assessing needs, risks and rights

Lee-Ann Fenge

INTRODUCTION

Community care has become a popular concept over the past 30 years and as Means and Smith (1998) suggest it has become *almost universally espoused as desirable for service users and a central pillar of policy of governments and politicians of all persuasions* (p2).

However, what is meant by the term 'community care' is far from clear. It is a contested concept with multiple meanings. Is it provided by lay people in an open setting (i.e. non-institutionalised care) which is most normally care by the family, or can it be seen as statutory support of user groups? To large organisations such as the NHS, any non-health service provision may be viewed as community care; therefore institutions run by local authorities constitute community care. Others may translate community care to mean de-institutionalisation.

What is 'community care'?

The debate about community care centres on relationships between the individual, the family and the state. Walker (1998) has sought to address this problem of defining community care by pointing out that it is easy for one person's community care to be another person's institutional care.

The term community care may therefore mean different things to different people, and no single definition exists. The White Paper *Caring for People* defines it in the following way:

> *Community Care means providing services and support which people who are affected by the problems of ageing, mental illness, mental handicap or physical or sensory disability need to be able to live as independently as possible in their own homes, or in 'homely' settings in the community.*

> (DoH, 1989, p3)

The question of who cares is important here, and much of the support provided is by 'informal' or unpaid carers. The subject of 'informal' care has been in the forefront of policy in recent years. A number of reasons have led to this, including concerns about demographic changes and who will care for the growing numbers of increasingly frail older people. It may be true to say that there has always been a 'mixed economy' of community care. Lewis (1999) suggests that *social care in the post war period, unlike health care, has always been a very mixed economy and arguably the family has always been the main provider* (p334). However, the remit of this chapter is not to explore the discourse around caring, but to explore in more depth issues involved in assessment such as the concepts of needs, rights and risks.

Care management

The role of the care manager is central to community care and to the assessment process. Care management and assessment were identified by the 1989 White Paper, *Caring for People*, as being *the cornerstone* of high quality care (Cmd. 849, para.1.11.).

Assessment is a key social work task. It can be seen as the preparation for *decision making* (Sinclair et al. 1995, cited Milner and O'Byrne, 1998). It is therefore important to look at the effectiveness of the decisions which come from the assessment process. As Milner and O'Byrne warn, *assessment has never been the scientific activity that many writers have pretended* (p8).

Indeed some writers suggest that the nature of social work is challenged by notions of post-modernity which leads to uncertainties about whether or not there are any *deep and unwavering principles which define the essence of its character and hold it together as a coherent enterprise* (Howe, 1994 p513).

Assessment does not occur in a vacuum, and as policy changes, the nature of assessment itself is altered. For example the policy on delayed discharge (DoH, 2003) and the single assessment process (DoH, 2002) have influenced the timescales that assessments must be undertaken in, as well as emphasising the collaborative nature of assessments. These policy developments, alongside Fair Access to Care (DOH, 2002) have also raised the importance of other factors within the assessment process such as an increasing emphasis on eligibility criteria and an associated awareness of 'risk'. Jordan (2004) suggests that the consequence of re-framing policy is that it focuses social work *on the assessment of resources and risks, despite the rhetoric of empowerment and inclusion* (p 10). Care managers are therefore faced with a tension between their professional values of 'user empowerment' and the restrictions posed by agency accountability and funding criteria (Fenge, 2001).

What are the skills of assessment?

Possible lack of clarity about what these skills are have, perhaps, led to a preoccupation with methods of intervention. Curnock and Hardiker (1979) suggest that methods then tend to influence the assessment, becoming a sort of 'practice theory'. Milner and O'Byrne (1998) also warn of the fact that social work has uncritically imported knowledge from other disciplines, stating that *borrowed knowledge from psychiatry and psychology has been the major influence on social work practice* (p5). Others have suggested that assessment within care management is further restricted by an emphasis on bureaucratic procedures which emphasises more procedural models of practice and the 'administrative' process (Lymbery, 2005, p154).

Assessment of need

Within community care policy, both policy and practice guidance refers to *needs-led* assessment, although the legislation does not provide any definition of what need might be. Local authorities are left with the power to decide what services might be provided to meet need. Section 47(1) of the *NHS and Community Care Act* states:

> *Where it appears to a local authority that any person for whom they may provide or arrange for the provision of community care services may be in need of any such services, the authority – (a) shall carry out an assessment of his/her needs for those services; and (b) having regard to the results of that assessment, shall decide whether his/her needs call for the provision by them of any such services.*

Need is therefore an undefined concept, and each local authority has much discretion in deciding how it will define and use the concept through the application of *eligibility criteria*. It is *consequently an unpredictable element, varying from locality to locality* (Mandelstam, 1999, p105). Problems arise as the concept of need presupposes that we have a common understanding of what human need is and that we can accurately assess need and provide resources to meet it (Dalrymple and Burke, 1995).

The concept of need itself is problematic, and has been used to denote 'individual need' as well as the wider 'needs of society'. This encompasses notions of individual versus collective need. Do we have a common understanding about what a need actually is?

Langen (1998) suggests that these two different concepts of need can lead to problems in societies where there are high levels of social inequality (p6). In these situations it may be difficult for a society to reconcile individual need, or to demand the need as identified by the state. This may then encourage society to view some needs as 'deserving' and some as 'undeserving' as one way of rationing available resources. The use of eligibility criteria to target need can be seen as a similar mechanism to deserving and undeserving of the Poor Law system. Therefore any discussion of need has to explore the social and political context in which the definition is constructed. It is a dynamic concept, which is contested in nature and open to many interpretations. In the post-war welfare state 'universalism' was a central theme – health, education, basic social security benefits and social services were available to everyone 'in need' (Langen, 1998).

How we assess need may depend to a large extent on how we approach the concept. Liss (1998) describes two different approaches to the assessment of need:

- **Tension need** – need is viewed as tension or a disequilibrium – needs are satisfied when tension is eliminated. If we assess need using the 'tension' approach we assess what people actually strive for.

- **Teleological need** – need in this context is related to a certain goal, and the need is a lack of something or a gap related to a certain goal. To assess using this approach is to assess what things are necessary to achieve a certain goal.

21

These different approaches will impact upon the solutions offered to service users in terms of responding to the definitions service users might use, versus professional definitions of what resource is required to meet a need.

Maslow's Hierarchy of Need (1954) suggests a teleological view of need in terms of the need to meet certain goals within a hierarchy of need.

1. Physiological needs – include the need for food, warmth, drink, sex, sleep, etc.

2. Safety needs – concerned with security, stability, and the avoidance of pain and physical damage through external forces.

3. Need for belonging and love – feeling secure when in close, intimate contact with others. According to Maslow these include: – one's territory, one's clan, one's gang, one's class and one's familiar working colleagues (p 44).

4. Esteem needs – having status and acceptance in one's group – satisfaction of these needs lead to feelings of self worth and confidence.

5. Need for self actualisation – the drive to self fulfilment and the expression of potentialities and capabilities.

6. Need for cognitive understanding – the understanding of the self and the external world.

According to Maslow the basic needs (physiological needs) must be met before the higher needs can be realised.

Assessing need using these two different approaches will give different results. Many different dimensions operate in the arena of needs assessment. At what point does a need become a want? How does the impact of rationing resources through eligibility criteria impact upon the way need is seen? What rights do service users have in having their needs met?

One model which may prove useful when we explore different definitions of need is Bradshaw's Taxonomy of Social Need (1972).

Bradshaw's Taxonomy of Social Need

Bradshaw (1972) suggests that the concept of 'social need' is inherent in the idea of social service, and *the history of the social services is the story of the recognition of social needs and the organisation of society to meet them* (p640).

Four classes of need can be used in the process of policy formation:

1. Normative need.

2. Felt need.

3. Expressed need.

4. Comparative need.

Normative need

Bradshaw defines normative need as that which:

> *The expert or professional, administrator or social scientist defines as need in any given situation.*

(p640)

A desirable standard is laid down and this is then compared with the standard that actually exists. The normative definition of need is subject to the value judgements of the 'expert'. In many situations 'expressed' or 'felt' need is not considered a valid indicator of need until it has been legitimised by an expert. The system of assessment within social service departments can be seen as a system in which 'experts' are actively involved in the assessment and prescription of services on behalf of service users. Within community care systems, the purchasing function does not tend to be financed directly by the 'consumer', but through taxes and social service allocation of resources, over which the individual service user has little control (Lewis et al. 1995). Briggs (1991) suggests that there is an inherent inequality in the 'helper-helped' relationship if one party controls the resources whilst the other party is in 'need'.

Felt need

In this situation, need is equated with want. Bradshaw suggests that:

> *Felt need is, by itself, an adequate measure of 'real need'. It is limited by the perception of the individual.*

(p641)

Felt need is therefore focused on people's subjective perceptions of need. It will also be influenced by the type of questions asked about how a need is felt, i.e. would you like / do you want / do you need.

It will also be influenced by comparisons people make with their peers and other groups.

Expressed need

According to Bradshaw (1972) people have an expressed need if they feel a need for a service and have requested or demanded that their need be met. He suggests that:

> *Expressed need or demand is felt need turned into action.*

(p641)

e.g. waiting lists in health service or housing departments. Expressed need may also be voiced by groups, voluntary organisations, political parties, etc, and pressure groups can be influential in identifying new needs. However, it is also important to remember that often the people most in need may have the greatest difficulty in expressing their needs.

Comparative need

A measure of comparative need is obtained by studying the characteristics of the population in receipt of a service. If some people are in receipt of a service and others in similar circumstances are not, then the latter are considered to be in need.

When the four classes of the taxonomy are applied to individuals, need may be identified as being present or absent by each definition in turn. As a result, individuals will be found to fall into one of 12 categories of need. However, criticisms of this model highlight the tension between the normative definition of need framed by policy makers and 'experts', and the felt or expressed needs of service users (Kemshall, 1984). These tensions may be compounded in a system in which care managers not only assess need but also act as 'purchasers' of care for the service user, they retain much control in the type of care received. The care manager and the social service departments in which they operate have ultimate control about who will and will not receive a service. As Means and Smith (1998) suggest:

> There is much talk of eligibility criteria and the priority matrix, as social service authorities continue to define ever more narrowly the number of people they claim they are able to provide a service for.
>
> (p120)

Risks and rights

Although the rhetoric of community care supports the idea of a needs-led assessment, Postle (2002) suggests that the context of care management is influenced by three main factors: restricted resources, operating within a market for care, and risk. Therefore alongside assessment of need, risk and the assessment of risk are key concerns for staff in social care organisations. The assessment of risk covers the difficult areas of 'protection', 'rights' and 'responsibilities'. Milner and Byrne (1998) suggest that the differing emphases on risks, needs and resources make it difficult for social work to develop an overarching framework for all their assessments. They also suggest that too much theory can be used oppressively, when it is used as if it were the truth for particular client systems. This also raises the issue of 'rights' to services and rights to take risks. It has been suggested that need and risk should not be central in determining welfare policy, but that notions of citizenship and rights should be paramount (Oliver, 1996).

According to Dickinson, 1981 (cited Kemshall and Pritchard, 1996), *life without risk would be sterile*. In our everyday lives we are all involved in elements of risk taking, but risk taking needs to be balanced against exposing ourselves and others to unnecessary harm and danger. Within practice, this translates to working with the conflicts between the rights of service users to take risks, the rights and needs of carers, workers and the general public. According to Parton (1996), risk has become the key criterion for targeting scarce resources, protecting the most vulnerable and making professionals and agencies accountable. This also raises important questions concerning the nature of risk such as should there be a right to take a risk, and is the law an appropriate mechanism for ensuring rights in relation to risk taking? (Titterton, 2005).

Risk and assessment of risk have now become a central component of the care manager's assessment as by the late 1990s *needs-led welfare was transformed into risk-led, positive welfare of the Third Way* (Kemshall, 2002, p40).

However, despite the term 'risk' being used within the arena of social care, it is difficult to find clear definitions or criteria about what is actually meant by this term. Pritchard (1997) suggests that the term 'vulnerable' is being increasingly used because of the increased concern about 'vulnerable adults', particularly in the arena of abuse. However, different organisations may define vulnerability differently, and again local resource availability may impinge on the definitions used to define risk as well as need.

Vulnerability

The notion of vulnerability is important. It suggests the need for protection. If an older person is considered to be vulnerable, taking risks may be actively discouraged because it is felt that the individual needs to be protected from danger.

For certain client groups, the impact of discrimination may increase the view of vulnerability and decrease the likelihood of risk taking. Conrad (1992) (cited Phillips, 1996) suggests that welfare institutions have tended to treat all their older clients as dependent and thus in a negative light, and this can lead to *justification for ever-increased intervention* (p135).

Recent legislation has offered increased protection to vulnerable adults in terms of their rights to be supported to make their own decisions. The recent Mental Capacity Act (2005) provides a statutory framework to empower and protect vulnerable people who are not able to make their own decisions. It makes clear who can make decisions, in which situations, and how they should go about this. Guidance on the Act is provided in a Code of Practice. Enactment of the Act is not expected until April 2007.

Five key principles underpin the Act.

- **A presumption of capacity** – every adult has the right to make his or her own decisions and must be assumed to have capacity to do so unless it is proved otherwise.

- **The right for individuals to be supported to make their own decisions** – people must be given all appropriate help before anyone concludes that they cannot make their own decisions.

- Individuals must retain **the right to make what might seem eccentric or unwise decisions**.

- **Best interests** – anything done for or on behalf of people without capacity must be in their best interests.

- Least restrictive intervention – anything done for or on behalf of people without capacity should be the **least restrictive of their basic rights and freedoms**.

The law already presumes capacity and the Act reasserts this principle, but also provides that anyone involved in someone's care/treatment can assess and conclude that the subject is incapacitated on the basis of *reasonable belief*.

The Act replaces current statutory schemes for enduring powers of attorney and Court of Protection with reformed and updated schemes.

The Act deals with the assessment of a person's capacity and acts by carers of those that lack capacity.

- **Assessing lack of capacity** – the Act sets out a single clear test for assessing whether a person lacks capacity to take a particular decision at a particular time – *a decision specific test*. No one can be labelled incapable as a result of a particular medical condition or diagnosis.

- **Best interests** – the Act provides a checklist of factors a decision-maker must work through in deciding what is in a person's best interests.

The future

The introduction of the single assessment process had led to a fundamental review of assessment practice. The recent introduction of the Single Assessment Process for Older People has had an impact on the dimensions of need, risks and rights within the assessment process. Annex D of the guidance talks in terms of the need for all health and social care systems to follow a common set of shared values, drawn from the *NHS Plan* and the *National Service Frameworks for Older People* (p7).

These should be:

- valuing carers and family members;

- valuing integrated and responsive services;

- valuing staff.

The Department of Health lists guidance as to which information the single assessment should gather under nine domains:

- user's perspective;

- clinical background;

- disease prevention;

- personal care and physical well-being;

- senses (vision, hearing);

- mental health;

- relationships;

- safety (including abuse);

- immediate environment and resources.

The role of the care manager has been central to the assessment process to date. However, the single assessment process allows for any professional within the wider multi-disciplinary team to lead the overview assessment. Glasby (2004) expresses concern that individual agencies may be unwilling to use validated assessment tools, and will not have the expertise or resources to develop their own. It has also been suggested that to be successful, the single assessment process needs to recognise the actual state of multi-disciplinary working, rather than an idealised vision of harmony (Cornes and Clough, 2004).

There is also a risk that more procedural mechanistic models of practice will down-play the skill involved in engaging with the service user's perspective, and this may be particularly relevant when looking at how the single assessment process is implemented. What skills are needed to support the service user in the 'authorship' of their needs and care package, and how will this be maintained under the new assessment arrangements? The use of formalised and objective assessment tools may lead to little engagement with the service user. Gorman (2000) warns against a focus on the technical aspects of work to the exclusion of the emotional and suggests that *such an approach denies care managers the opportunity to meet individual needs in a holistic way and to make empowering practice a reality* (p15).

The onus rests on the worker's ability to engage in this discursive process. It is more than just listening to the surface representations of self, which may become apparent in more formalised question driven formats of assessment. It is an interpretation, alongside the older person, of the 'meaning' within their story (Schindler, 1999). By focusing the assessment on the service user's 'voice' and the story they have to tell, older people may be increasingly empowered within the assessment process (Fenge, 2001). Yet ultimately resource availability will continue to play a central role in the care management process and the way in which individual needs, rights and risks are perceived.

Chapter 3

Performance management: causes and effects and their impact on community care

Jason Marshall

INTRODUCTION

The improvement, through greater efficiency and effectiveness, of Social Services departments has been sought ever increasingly over the last 25 years. From the speeches of senior politicians to the decisions from team managers, there is an undercurrent of constant expectation that more can be done, more flexibly and providing greater choice (Community Care, 2004b), often with less money, time, and with greater threats for not achieving (Milburn, 2002). This is despite a rising population overall, a recent rise of 77% in the provision of Home Care (from 1992 – 2002) and growing numbers of disabled people needing support (based on those claiming Disability Living Allowance rising 25% in the last five years) (Social Trends, 2004).

In this chapter the issues around procuring resources and providing services will be looked at through the prism of performance management. The discussion will look at the political and ideological make up of current welfare policy and practice, how this leads to the type of performance management we have today, the management of social care and the external pressures placed on the budget managers.

Particular attention will be paid to an irreconcilable divergence of the aims of Social Services as stated in standards, performance management assessment and political aims by the government, and the work which can effectively be carried out by the department in which I work. Issues of management methods and the performance management agenda, and their effects on user choice and social work practice, will be analysed. Questions will be raised about ideological consistency and effective provision of care. Examples will be given of the fractured and incomplete work this allows for.

The path – shifts that paved the way

The present Labour government came to power on a platform of stable public spending and widespread reform of the public sector (Cole, 1999), including the basis for and the manner of welfare provision. This can be seen as a partial continuation of new right ideas about how the role of the public sector needed to be subsidiarist – minimised so as not to encourage dependency (Esping-Anderson, 1990). But while Margaret Thatcher herself promised to 'roll back' the state, Labour promised reform, improvement and carefully directed investment while the Chancellor, Gordon Brown, kept a firm hand on the budget. They would ensure that no charges of excessive public spending could be levelled at them while efficient, improved services were supporting those most in need and socially excluded – a subsidiarist welfare state, yet expandable under the correct conditions. Spending would be controlled in a regulated rather than liberated market in welfare, as the economy remained stabilised, the global capitalist economy accepted (Driver and Martell, 1998).

The introduction of the market in welfare and the current ideological basis for welfare itself is generally regarded as occurring in the 1970s with the end of the Keynsian post-war 'consensus'. A move away from the grand statist welfare state to an alternative model was needed, to respond to the needs of a shifting global economy and changed world (Taylor-Goodby et al., 1999; Fulcher, 1999; Hutton, 1995; Ellison and Pierson, 1998). Favoured in the polls in the late 1970s, the Conservatives presented the most popular way forward. With inspiration from a variety of 'new right' thinkers, including high ranking members of her own party, Margaret Thatcher, and John Major, as her successor, presided over massive changes in welfare ideology and provision. These changes, their effect, for example, on the unemployed and on the role of women, are well documented elsewhere (e.g. Daly and Lewis, 1998). The continued spiralling of welfare costs (Finlayson, 1994) despite these measures cannot be fully explored here, but this is an important aspect in later analysis. What will be looked at here will be the ideology that drove them and the legacy – the establishment of a new welfare paradigm and a new consensus (Driver and Martell, 1998; Harris and McDonald, 2000).

Changes since the Community Care Act

Following the implementation of the NHS and Community Care Act 1990, in 1993, according to the White Paper Caring for People, the aim was to provide *the best form of care* to meet their needs and maximise independence and choice for service users (Department of Health, 1989, p4–5). A key component was a service focus on those with *the greatest needs* (ibid, p5); some have argued that this meant only those in greatest need, as eligibility was reduced (Daly and Lewis, 2000; Cole, 1999). The state monopoly of provision was replaced by a welfare market. The competition between providers as they battled for the business of social care was presented as a means to force prices down and quality up. Consumer choice and the pursuit of profit would lead to satisfactory outcomes for both sides of the transaction (Ellison and Pierson, 1998). It was envisaged that in this way the aims of the White Paper would be met.

A *flexible, cost effective, post-Fordist model of service delivery* (Harris and MacDonald, 2000, p53) was an economic requirement for the Conservative administration as it sought to support the new post-Keynesian welfare market (Taylor-Goodby et al., 1999). Home care, for example, expanded through massive development of the independent sector (Smith et al., 1995) and local authorities were required to spend the majority of their budgets on such contract-based external services (Postle, 2002). Other requirements of a post-Fordist model were the decentralisation of budgets and control (Harris and MacDonald, 2000; Driver and Martell, 1998).

Spending, along with the quality of remaining Local Authority services, were measured together for the first time with the introduction of Joint Reviews, carried out by the Audit Commission and The Social Services Inspectorate. Just as the owner of a private business may promote efficient productivity with rewards, local authorities were required to prove they were businesslike (Ball and Peters, 2000). The role of social workers had been altered to fit a new pattern of care purchasing, with management structures (local control, devolved budgets and contract-based provision) to suit. The effects of this managerial shift and later consolidation of these ideas will be explored further on in this chapter.

The new Labour project – a careful construction

When Labour came to power there were no intentions to turn the clock back. There was a need to find a vote-winning compromise, distinct from perceived failings of the last Labour administration, between the old-fashioned protective welfare state and the more subsidiarist marketplace with its purportedly lower tax burden. Not raising the basic rate of Income Tax was a key election pledge and the Chancellor, Gordon Brown, promised economic stability:

I had to get us out of the stop-go, boom-bust cycle that had dominated our economy for 40 or 50 years.

(quoted in MacKenzie, 2004)

However, there was a need to satisfy the more left-leaning elements of the party, so promises of developments in welfare were made.

But this was not going to be a simple giving exercise. A further requirement of post-Fordist economic management is for economic forces, state forces and welfare provision to be linked (Harris and MacDonald, 2000). This can be seen in New Labour policy as recipients, while being entitled to benefits as of right (to support, as defined by the State), were required to accept greater responsibilities (of the individual to the State). Support was and continues to this day to be couched in terms of a way back in to work and in to the economy (see, for example *Financial Times*, 2004). Social welfare was not going to be just about tackling hardship but, to meet the economic needs of the state, subordinate to conditions for wealth creation (Jessop, 1994, cited in Harris and MacDonald, 2000).

There are connections between this theoretical framing and the model of the State's role and welfare provision proposed by sociologist Anthony Giddens in his Third Way theories. Giddens (2000) proposes (amongst much more in many writings) that new *strategies and institutions* are needed to deliver the support of a welfare state (ibid, p45). Welfare was needed for social justice, but also needed to be a process to self-actualisation, rather than an end product (echoed on the political right by Whelan, 1999).

Under Tony Blair, 'New' Labour positioned itself with Giddens: beyond, rather than just between left and right. Welfare would not remain a matter of collective support – dispensing benefits, but aim to empower people, to enable them to participate in productive life within managed capitalism (Mouzelis, 2001). The capital of welfare would also be more tightly monitored under a new inspection regime. In the 1998 White Paper Modernising Social Services, new targets to ensure *quality and efficiency improvements* (Department of Health, 1998) were promised.

The growth of choice

Another key theme, continued through successive governments, has been increasing choice. This is an aim which has been present from the 1990 Caring for People White Paper right up to the present, with the imminent publication of the Adult Social Services Green Paper (Community Care, 2004b). Choice was touted as a natural consequence of the market in services and individuals have been given greater choice with the introduction, expansion and strong promotion of Direct Payments (Bevans, 2004). But Social Services departments are facing not only more expensive provision such as that for residential care, but an increase in disability and in population (Social Trends, 2004). Growth in Social Services spending has dropped to 1.3% a year (Community Care, 2004b). So to fulfil the improvement aims of Modernising Social Services, nearly £3 billion was made available through the Social Services Modernisation Grant but:

> *This is not more money to provide more of the same... The Modernisation Fund money will be tied to conditions and targets, to ensure that the extra funds deliver the necessary service improvements.*

> (Department of Health, 1998, p4)

Modernisation, as prescribed by the Department of Health, is mandatory - measurable achievement a precondition. How the controls and limitations of this framework and current policy lead and confine the actions of local authorities, and how they contradict yet rely on certain ideas present in the market economy (and Third Way theory) will now be explored in more detail.

The dominance of performance management

Performance Indicators (PIs), as a part of the imposed performance management system, have been in place in Local Authorities since 1997; in Adult Services social work since April 2003. They form a part of the Department of Health's Performance Assessment Framework (PAF) (Department of Health, 2002). This monitoring identifies:

> *how well the council delivers their services...considers how well the council is run, as this will impact on how they deliver their services in the future.*

> Audit Commission (2002)

It is an essential tool in managing services and a key component of the government's modernisation agenda (Audit Commission, 2002). They feed information to the Department of Health which produces lists of authorities and their 'star ratings'. These are widely publicised and the poor performing authorities have been 'named and shamed'.

As local authorities strive to produce favourable statistical outcomes, it is clear that satisfying the needs of particular Performance Indicators has also played a major part in forming service delivery priorities for Social Services departments (Burnham, 2004). This is evident in the measures taken to effect speedy hospital discharges (see, for example, Kumar, 2004; Hayes, 2004) with undoubtedly some positive effects and financial support from the Department of Health. However, concerns have been expressed about the safety of such new procedures (Healthcare Commission, 2004, cited by Kenny, 2004).

While the statutory context here is one of an Act of Parliament (the Community Care (Delayed Discharges) Act 2004) and financial reward, the pressures brought to bear for less specific achievements (such as encouraging giving greater numbers of people help to live at home and other efficiency factors such as acceptable unit costs of different forms of service) are less clearly identified. New projects, initiatives and whole services have been developed in my authority and, for each one, there has been a specific performance management goal in sight. Performance Indicators have been noted as driving service delivery priorities (Tilbury, 2004). Money has been found for a specific grant for offering Direct Payments only, placing the method of service delivery, and Performance Indicator attainment, above the overall budgetary prioritisation for those most in need.

Such developments are generally positive in their outcomes for the people they serve (total number helped also being counted). From a developmental point of view, however, the changes are in danger of being short lived. A specific budget was set up to enable hospital discharges to be effected rapidly, even with intensive care packages (another Performance Indicator). The money was ring-fenced to pay for the care in the current financial year, but the following year it will be just as expensive and need to come out of a budget from somewhere.

Effects of peformance management

In my authority there have been two noticeable effects in two separate, distinct areas. They illustrate the micro-effects of Performance Indicator-led services, so are worthy of explanation. Firstly, it can affect outcomes for service users and create exclusion. In my authority, the meals-on-wheels service is currently delivered by one, bulk contracted provider. The subsidy required has been negotiated down to its optimum level, so for every meal subsidised, a key Performance Indicator can gain an efficient point. The delicate cost-balance would be upset by subsidising another provider at higher cost, which they will not do. But the SSD-funded service has no established non-English cultural menu and not even a simple choice for vegetarians. Therefore, a person seeking a non-English, ethnically or personal-ethically appropriate service is not counted – they are not actually helped.

Second, it can fail to recognise work achieved that is entirely congruent with the purpose of social work. If the work with an individual is completed, they are closed to the service and it is not counted. That is to say, if a short term piece of work has led to an individual moving 'through' the service, having been helped to regain their independence and they no longer require a social worker, this is of no Performance Indicator value (unless it falls within the sample period, when we have been warned not to close cases for this reason).

Disadvantages of performance management

Finally, there are some general, apparently opposed indicators. Burnham (2004) mentions the conflict of settling children (good for children and one indicator), yet having to move them to try to achieve this ('bad' for another). In my service we have a requirement to place as few people as possible in long term care (leading to a good rating). Yet the ultimate success of this policy would mean that the few for whom there is no alternative would, for that very reason, be expensive to place (bad rating). This is not helped by the residential placements target figure being less than the cost of any placement I have made in the recent past.

As departments get wiser, the statistics improve because the methods of compiling them improve. Without analysis, 'awareness' begins to amount to 'improvement':

> *a greater awareness of performance management ... has resulted in a 'significant overall improvement' in the performance of councils.*

> (Community Care, 2003, p6 parentheses in original)

This does not amount to better services.

Social work and managerialism in local Social Services

> *Local Authority Social Services departments have been reformed and now operate by means of management approaches borrowed from the private sector.*

> (Harlow, 2003, p29)

The requirement on local authorities as a whole, as well as Social Services departments, to operate along the lines of a private business fits with both the stipulated aims of Conservative administrations (Ellison and Pierson, 1998) and the New Labour third way-influenced post Conservative cautious policies (Postle, 2002). The performance management agenda originated in several initiatives through the 1980s, recalled by Lupton (1992), with the Social Services Inspectorate launching 'Key Indicators' in 1988 (ibid). Lupton notes that these were not intended to be the sole source of data for comparative analysis, more a prompt for further research into service qualities. However, the New Labour regime has run with this idea in a less qualitatively rigorous and most manipulable form. Only a managerial-technicist approach will provide data that fits with its administration obsessed (Driver and Martell, 1998) performance management process, where external evaluations will be key (Lupton, 1992).

Tsui (2004) states that this requires the roles of managers to be placed as central to the success of the organisation and their knowledge is dominant (or in the case of performance management, the knowledge they are told to value by national government). They add that managers here will tend to count instead of judge and that quality is equated with documentation. Harris (1998) went further in his earlier article, suggesting that social work had begun undergoing *proceduralisation* and *commodification* (p858). The placing of financial constraints at the centre of interpersonal work, the deferment of professional discretion to budgetary considerations and increased direction from above were proposed as leading to an end of the autonomous bureau-professional. Lymbery (1998) and McDonald et al. (2000) concur, there is a separation from decision processes and subordination of social worker judgements to management definitions of effectiveness.

On analysis of my role in day to day social work, I can see Tsui and Cheung's suspicions in action, but for this to lead to Harris's feared undermining of my role would require the high level of monitoring. Sadly, the demands of the former, along with case supervision, appear to fill my manager's time so entirely that the degree of monitoring has not increased in the slightest. Decisions as to whether support should be provided are financial ones in the main, but my hours are filled with interpersonal work where successful outcomes do not have quantitative measures applied (although I have been congratulated on avoiding spending). However, this is partly due to my role as a specialist worker with a small, complex caseload. The procedural aspects arise, but the 'turnover' of clients in order to attain high levels of 'productivity' is not consistently required. My colleagues in the main team certainly feel this pressure. Quality of work, along with the professional role and morale of staff, is widely thought to be suffering (McDonald et al., 2000; Jordan and Jordan, 2000; Healy, 2002).

The management definition of effectiveness is encapsulated in Performance Management. Government priorities tell authorities that between inspections, nothing else matters. Eligibility criteria take procedural decisions away from us (Jordan and Jordan, 2000; McDonald et al., 2000), but what of the quality and types of services that users expect and wish for? This will be analysed after looking briefly at the coercion and encouragement from central government.

Incentives and support from central government, and its absence

The increases from the Modernisation Fund go to those that manage little well (Jordan and Jordan, 2000), yet this is, in itself, a contradiction in policy. This requirement to perform well with little or normal spending leads to extra money being made available for improvements. Yet it would seem contrary to sound business sense to throw good money at an efficient service, serving people well. Good services are having money forced on them while other key services suffer underfunding, owing to *performance management from the centre* (Community Care, 2004c).

The basic expense of providing seems ignored, an assumption of inefficiency comes in. Struggling services not serving people well cannot improve when they will not get more money for core services. As Janet Lewis reflected on this change of trust: *no-one could be trusted to do anything right* (Lewis, 2000). She goes on to ask where is the evidence that this kind of treatment of departments and staff works? It has a direct effect on the service it can then provide. The communities and individuals the government is ostensibly trying to help are left with services the government itself is condemning. Where is the support at these times for those most vulnerable, as espoused by the social justice elements of Third Way thinking?

Meanwhile, the pressure continues. A recent report – by accountants – for the Treasury (the Gershon Report) states confidently that £650 million can be found in efficiency savings in the national Social Care budget (HM Treasury, 2004).

User's perspectives and issues of quality and equality

Quality in Social Services is not measured by the people who are its intended beneficiaries. The setting of priorities, the diversion of funds and resources take place out of the public domain (Sumner, 2004) as do decisions on the withdrawal of support for 'failing' authorities. As I have demonstrated above, this can remove choice.

The publicly available information does not ask any questions about the quality of services to minorities (Lupton, 1992; both at the time of writing and at present), is objective and scientific based on the positions of those who hold the power in the user/professional relationship (Thompson, 1999). Beresford and Branfield (2004) add that policies are driven by knowledge held by professionals rather than users, additionally pointing out the most glaring evidence of exclusive, 'expert' driven changes – no less than the forthcoming Green Paper on adult services was set out by the Department of Health with no consultation with service users.

There is suspicion that the overall 'market' is not necessarily a good thing either, as well as policies which prevent its use. In the words of one service user, writer and user representative:

Choice means nothing without working to improve standards.

(Heng, 2004, p23)

Heng adds that shifts in staffing means poorer continuity and trust for users. This is not heeded when one sees that the department sets its own priorities for commissioning (such as the Home Care scenario, below). When a user has apparently maximum control, employing staff with Direct Payments funds, my department offers only a fixed sum per hour, with which users have to find workers from the same pool as every other understaffed care provider. Over ten years on from the introduction of the market, questions over the centrality of choice have even been echoed by the Audit Commission (2004). It suggests responsiveness in place of choice, where it cannot be achieved. Service users consulted for the report said that overall they simply wanted relevant services to be of better quality.

The list of Performance Indicators includes some under the sub-heading *quality of services for users and carers*. They actually refer to quantitative measures of speed, event occurrence and existence of paperwork. There is no evidence of what works well with people, what people value and how they felt – no real qualitative measures (Tilbury, 2004). The Performance Indicator framework simply provides evidence that SSDs are working hard (Lewis, 2001) and striving to be effective in those areas measured. Users find the resulting star ratings vague (Batty, 2002).

There is a key element of Third Way policy left out of this system. With its enabling, independence promoting slant, no indicator exists to demonstrate how effective this type of empowering support is. No-one is measuring the success rate of people helped to pass through the system and to become active, non-dependent citizens.

The assumption of a market

A key aim of the changes introduced since the early 1990s was the devolution of budgetary control to local care purchasers, who could in turn benefit from a range of services where market forces would keep provision at a high quality and reasonably priced. For several reasons, this has simply not happened. It is proposed here that the assumption of a market is a key element in the restriction of creative, user-centred purchasing of care, the restriction of choice in welfare provision and a general failure of Third Way policies. There follows two short micro-analyses based on my personal experience of purchasing and the local context.

A simple example is that there is no residential care for people under 65 in my county, only nursing care, forcing us to pay for services we do not require. Many care agencies checked and approved by the contracts section are continually over-subscribed, all have recruitment problems. This pales next to difficulties my management colleagues have had in pushing the hourly average cost of home care to lower (that is, minimum wage plus around £3.50) levels.

My local authority runs the most expensive (and for my team colleagues, most trusted) Home Care service in the county which was seen to contribute to an unfavourable Performance Indicator rating for both the unit cost of each hour of home care and the number of intensive packages provided. The answer was to make the in- house service a specialist intensive and introductory provider, with stable packages being passed to cheaper, long-term, block-purchased agency care. The tenders were taken up by two agencies, but costs rose as they encountered recruitment problems at pre-set wage levels, then one folded – unable to recruit and cope. This seized up the in-house service as all packages were taken on board again. Harnessing the market to our advantage failed.

The insistence on market methods in the context of an absent market demonstrates a failing to operate under consistently post-Fordist management. New monopolies of independent services (Holman, 2004) are being created (or, as above, attempted) to replace rather than improve on the old local authority monopolies, under extensive contracts. This clearly runs against the very reason why the market was thrown open and maintained, although it successfully reinforces centralised decision-making on how to meet needs, again distancing users and social workers from decision-making, as discussed above. Yet there are community support elements of Third Way thinking which are not addressed by using mass providing agencies instead of small, focused local ones (Holman, 2004; Jordan and Jordan, 2000).

Effects on practitioners

So when there is no market or competition for care and social workers are left to forage among the leftover capacity, when more people than ever come to Social Services needing support, and money has to be spent to meet specific targets, when target prioritisation overrides need and we are always being reminded of the importance of something we do not value (or sometimes even understand), the effect on social work practitioners is beyond measure. As Postle (2002) pointed out, the tensions between interpersonal work and the management of limited financial resources can affect workers' professionalism. Sumner (2004) adds that this tension may affect social workers internally as well – asking if our perspectives on needs suffer *distortion* when seen next to service management needs. Add to that the powerful, unfair, nonsensical and devaluing process of perform-ance management in its present form, and the promise of scrapping the whole process (as implied by Letwin, 2004) seems appealing.

Conclusion

Welfare budgets failed to fall with successive changes in welfare entitlement and provision (Cole, 1999; Jordan and Jordan, 2000). Spending on meeting needs, not necessarily cre-ative or highly efficient – just reliable, has to continue. It may not fit with a self-empowering, return to work, socially responsible model, nor support the needs of the broader economy, but it is still widely required.

Throughout this chapter, connections have been made between socio-economic policy and welfare. Here is a comparison: performance management encourages short-term specula-tive movements in capital (Healy, 2002; Jordan and Jordan, 2000), as does the global economy it functions within (Kuttner, 2000). However, this is a specific problem which Giddens (2000) identifies as an obstacle to stable economic policy, and I will add, national welfare economics. Policing the New Labour social care agenda and economic factors have become so strong that supposed principles have been forgotten. The social justice ele-ments of Third Way thinking appear as 'bolted-on' (Hutton, 1995, p46) as with previous governments, where economics actually take priority. But the reasons, when all these con-flicting ideas are implemented at once, are clear. The Third Way is an unstable compound, with honourable goals but means that date from another time.

There are elements of the *stampede to emphasise obligations* that predate this Labour gov-ernment (Daly and Lewis, 2000, p294) which could be said to fit with what the disabled may need and people want – support to get (back) to work, for example. There are more old ideas in Third Way thinking. Welfare within the market is certainly not new, nor is the emphasis on individual responsibilities or communities helping themselves (Jordan and Jordan, 2000). The preventative measures and end-oriented process of welfare is similarly not its exclusive domain. Where these ideas truly originated is probably hard to say as all have been around for many years. New Labour's take on Third Way thinking fails to bring them together because, as things stand and as described above – they are not compatible.

One only has to see the political right shifting in to Labour's middle ground to see a new consensus in formation. From the means of and purpose for delivering welfare, to the Shadow Chancellor's boasts of spending plans (in education, at least) equal to Labour's, no less (Letwin, 2004)! Meanwhile, the Tory leader makes no promises of tax cuts, despite years of complaining of 'stealth' taxes (Whitford, 2003). Welfare is expensive. At least both parties realise that. While the Tories may tap in to discontent in public services by *cutting bureaucracy* (Letwin, 2004), Labour continue with trying to tackle social evils with old medicine in a new bottle.

Looking ahead

What of prevention? Jones (2002) feels it is nowhere to be seen while the state is preoccupied with keeping the cost of exclusion to a minimum. It is certainly absent from the Performance Indicators (which, to support Jones's argument, do indeed create a push downwards in costs); it would be difficult to measure anyway. This is where the trust that Lewis (2000) spoke of is absent. If we are to support people to be non-dependent, to avoid services, even, and if it cannot be measured, we need to be trusted. I see little of that, but little free time on the part of managers to check my work for 'high' levels of performance either. There is too much being done to rationalise and objectively evaluate it all. Our most important work takes place between the statistics. There lies one real strength of the profession.

Chapter 4

The older person's social care and the enabling service

Keith Brown

INTRODUCTION

The National Health Service (NHS) and Community Care Act of 1990 and the gradual policy adjustments which prepared for it after 1988 (Robinson and Le Grand, 1994) had clear implications for the care of disabled and dependent older persons in terms of funding, decision-making, responsibility for care, and professional roles. The outcomes experienced by older people and their families are less clear and this chapter will attempt to explore some of the implications of social policy for the recipients of services.

The care of older people is located in the contested ground between the values of free market individualism and the politico-economic imperative of central control of public spending (George and Wilding, 1994; Hills, 1997) between social and health care (Twigg, 1997; Redfern, 1998), and between the conflicting power claims of professional management and the medical and allied professions (Harrison and Pollitt, 1994). The needs of older people may therefore provide a sharpened focus for analysis of the interplay of ideologies and interests within care provision and its implications for recipients.

It is not intended to take an historical perspective, but to select particular aspects of the ideology behind the reforms of the late 1980s and early 1990s which seem to bear especially on the relationship between older people and the organisation and control of health and social care.

The politico-ideological background

The main doctrinal assumptions, discussed by George and Wilding (1994) on which the neo-liberal-capitalist welfare reforms of the Thatcher government were based may be summarised as follows.

- The welfare state is economically damaging because it increases public spending and therefore the tax burden of the productive individual and of competitive business. In doing so it reduces enterprise, incentive and economic growth and so reduces the wealth of all levels of society including the very poor.

The emphasis on productive elements in society targets, for reduction of expenditure, groups who are unavoidably unproductive including older and disabled people. An

:rease in national wealth, it is argued, will improve the wellbeing of all and so issues of citizenship and social justice are subservient to growth in the economy (Dean, 1996).

- The welfare state creates a dependency culture and thereby impedes the entrepreneurial independence of outlook on which GB plc depends for its competitive edge.

The 'dependency culture' concept in relation to older people implies that families have come to see care of older relatives as the duty of the state and should now be asked to take back a responsibility they have avoided. In fact families, principally women, have cared for the majority of older persons (Hills, 1997) but the changing nature of the family, especially through increased divorce and serial marriage and the expectation that women work, is increasing the need for state support.

- The welfare state is intrinsically expansionary and resistant to politico-economic control.

With regard to health care, the expansion of medical technology and tradition of professional autonomy have been seen as a major inflationary factor, as well as a culture of increased expectation and demand for medical intervention as an individual social right. The resultant government policy has included managerialisation of the NHS in order to challenge professional power on behalf of government and to introduce a framework of measurement as a basis for rational, transparent decision-making.

Clarke and Newman (1998) argue that this has resulted in a new power struggle between managers and government and reduced democratic accountability. Vulnerable groups, defined as *wicked issues*, are problematic in this scenario because their needs are complex and rarely measurable in output terms and they tend to cross organisational boundaries. They cannot be defined in terms of core business so have low priority in the ethos of rational management (Clarke and Newman, 1998; Harrison and Pollitt, 1994; Clarke, 1998).

- Political planning of the economy is both impossible and damaging to the natural and efficient operations of the market. The free market knows best and without it, as in the centrally controlled welfare system, inefficiency and waste are inevitable.

Applied to the NHS where there is no direct purchaser-consumer, this principle has resulted in a quasi-market that has been seen as creating more administrative waste and discontinuity of services, though its benefits have been an increased transparency of cost issues and emphasis on quality improvement (Robinson and Le Grand, 1994).

- State paternalism towards the individual, however altruistic and whether administered through professionals or bureaucracy, is always an untenable intrusion into the right to freedom from interference, the only admissible freedom. The consumer knows best and must be freed to make choices in the welfare market.

Conflicting needs and rights

The resultant mix of tight political control of resources and economic freedom of market forces, which is linked with individuated rights and consumer-led services, has been seen as the origin of tensions and contradictions in the welfare policy reforms of the Thatcher government (Morgan, 1998; Clarke and Newman, 1998). The creation of self-governing, but budget-limited, NHS Trusts contains the conflicting elements of lack of democratic accountability through dispersal of power and yet tighter financial control from the centre.

The attempt to identify a consumer who has real choices in order for an internal market in health and social care to be self-regulating has resulted in the acceptance of a quasi-market compromise with socially and organisationally divisive consequences which may reduce the cost-efficiency and consumer orientation which were its main overt aims (Morgan, 1998; Clarke and Newman, 1998). The creation of new demand for services, inherent both in competition for patients in the primary care sector and in the systematisation of care management and need assessment, is concurrent with reduction of the means to meet demand and increased public awareness of rationing.

All these issues are problematic in rendering operative what is a fundamental dichotomy (Clarke and Newman, 1998; Bartlett et al., 1994; Morgan, 1998).

It is self-evident that state financial resources are finite. Rationing is inherent to the safety net concept of the welfare state (Morgan, 1998; Dean, 1996; Clarke and Newman, 1998). That the limit of those resources is likely soon to be exceeded by an uncontrollable welfare demand has been effectively countered. Hills (1997), from a survey of research findings and international comparisons, shows that the British welfare state is relatively economical and able to sustain such *upward pressures on welfare spending* as might be expected in the next 50 years. In particular, the NHS compares well in cost-effectiveness with most of Europe and the United States. Morgan (1998) asks in similar vein, *is 7.1% of GDP really an adequate amount to be spending on our health care*?

However, Hill does link his optimistic view of future resources to economic growth and it is not certain how spreading recession as a result of market collapse in East Asia might impact on Western economies (Ricupero, 1998; Shipman, 1998). Neither does he deny that the future of welfare provision is problematic given the conflicting political imperatives already mentioned.

That welfare spending is out of control and a danger to the health of the economy might be construed as a political truth and as such informs policy as part of a new political consensus, called by Clarke and Newman (1998) *the Thatcher settlement*. The liberal-capitalist doctrine that public spending increases individual and corporate taxation and so saps enterprise and economic growth (George and Wilding, 1994), the foundation of the welfare reforms of the Conservative governments (Butler, 1994) appears, in modified form, to underpin the fiscal and welfare policies of New Labour. There remains a commitment to at least hold taxation constant, and initiatives such as the proposed NHS Trust mergers for example, are justified on the grounds of cost cutting (Morgan, 1998).

Implications for dependent groups

The emphasis has changed. The concerns remain the same and are the all-pervasive background to organisational and professional decision-making in health and social care and especially to the support of long-term dependent groups such as older people. Despite Hills' debunking of the myth of the *demographic time bomb* (1997), the perceived problem of the increasing burden of older people, surviving to frail old age in greater numbers, continues to define the elderly in a negative, pejorative way.

Older people have been disadvantaged by the intensification and strategic development of rationing within the welfare reforms in several ways. The purchaser/provider split, which deepened the divide between health care and Social Services through the mechanism of conflicting budgetary needs, redefined the dependent older person as the bed blocker. The need for NHS Trusts to show optimum use of beds and the managerial concentration on outputs rather than outcomes has focused healthcare attention on earliest possible discharge and questioned the rationale for longer than average hospitalisation (Clarke and Newman, 1998; Jones, 1998). Clarke and Newman (1998) describe the role of the NHS Trust Manager as focusing on the requirement to manage demand, and see the broader management debates around bed blocking as a direct result of the emphasis on the measurable which derives from the output definition of efficiency.

Social service departments, by contrast, intent on operationalising the policy of a needs rather than provision led service, have a requirement for a slower process to allow for tailor-made care packages to be created for each user (Lewis and Glennerster, 1996). It is in this area of policy-created culture conflict that the tension between the directives both to create an enabling consumer empowering service, to cut costs and to increase measurable efficiency, that has implications for vulnerable groups and for interprofessional working, can most clearly be seen.

The role of care manager in assessing individual need, and planning and organising support, is both enabling and gatekeeping. It is also operating in a process designed to maximise consumer input into decision-making, and control has clearly been devolved to that recipient/professional interface. Mayo (1994) describes the difference of perspective between health and social services concerning at what point assessment should be carried out. For care managers it is important that the assessment is valid and remains so, as far as is possible, over time. Waiting for the consumer to reach a state of some stability is a necessity, both to ensure that the right decision is made and to limit costs.

Social *vs* health care

For the hospital, the imperative is to discharge from the bed at the earliest possible moment because, as Clarke and Newman point out, output not outcome is the measure of managerial efficiency, and a longer than average stay is a measurable cost that is not linked directly to an output. The managerialisation of the NHS is explained, by both Clarke and Newman (1998) and Harrison and Pollitt (1994), as an attempt to control health spending by reducing the ability of professionals to demand limitless funding for their prescribed treatments. In the hinterland between social and health care there is scope for vulnerable people to be reclassified in order that they become the responsibility of a different budget-holder.

In a needs-led social service, based on the complexity of care management operating in a dual role as gatekeeper and social worker, and directed to prioritise care in the home, and a managerialised and output orientated health service, interprofessional collaboration between the services becomes problematic. The climate of rationing and competition intensifies a fundamental conflict of interests (Mayo, 1994; Jones, 1998; Twigg, 1997).

Consequencs for older people's care

The tightening of the criteria for hospital care to prioritise acute medical care and give a low priority to higher dependency, slower turnover, less medicalised health care need has effectively placed care of the older person largely outside the universal element of the welfare state (Redfern, 1998; Jones, 1998). Twigg, (1997), discussing the phenomenon of the social, i.e. not medical care, points out that health care is free at the point of delivery whilst social care is means tested and contributory, or indeed, seen as a private concern. There is a political as well as a managerial organisational agenda.

Jack (1998) discusses Care in the Community in relation to the anti-institution consensus that defines institutions as buildings, and as always and exclusively depersonalising and debilitating, i.e. institutionalising in their outcomes. He identifies a diminishment of choice consequent to the closure of local authority residential provision and the capping of local government spending, which led to predominantly private or voluntary sector provision of residential care with no obstacle to *merger and marginalisation of the small provider*. Jones (1998) also claims that local authority funding of the private sector has led to closure of small homes and favoured monopolistic consortia. Mayo (1994) and Jack (1998) challenge the definition of community that excludes residence in a building other than the family home and is dependent on an idealistic conception of mutually supportive membership based on geographical location.

The politically plausible argument for the closure of NHS and Local Authority long stay provision is therefore challenged on the grounds of inaccurate definitions used to create a simplistic dualism, *Institutional care bad. Community care good* (Jack, 1998). Older persons have, as a result, less choice.

The consequence of the transfer of older person's care first to social care and then to the private sector has been that residential homes are now required to provide for highly dependent and frail people, mainly older persons, although their experience was gained with younger, fit disabled groups (Redfern, 1998). Jones (1998) raises concern over a loss of expertise, built up since the early criticisms of institutional care within local authority care of older people, and the move to inappropriate private provision. The increased levels of need and dependency being met outside hospitals, both in residential and home care, it is argued, are falling on carers with little training and experience and with little control or support. Jack (1998) points out that the task of 'tending' has been devalued as personal care has become low status manual work. The consequence for standards of care, when low status leads to low morale and sense of personal worth, seems likely to be an inevitable decline.

The belief that individual freedom consists exclusively of freedom from interference by the state, negative freedom, resulted in measures that sought to establish individuated rights rather than collective rights enforceable by virtue of membership in a particular community (Nettleton and Burrows, 1998). The individual as a consumer of health and social care was to be given the right of choice through the purchaser/provider split which established a quasi-market in health care, and through GP fund holding. Providers would be in competition with each other and league tables would ensure that GPs could choose on behalf of their patients, consultants and hospitals that proved to be most effective (Harrison and Pollitt, 1994).

Social Services were also given a purchaser role in respect of residential and home care services. Again, the individual, once need had been established and defined, was to have choice exercised through a professional, in this case a Care Manager. The choice is between parallel services, not whether a service should be funded. The professional gate-keeper, within the constraints of appeals systems, is the effective consumer (Paton, 1994).

Concerns for the vulnerable

Individuated rights assume that citizens are capable of and able to exercise them. Jones (1998) identifies the problem of families and older persons who may not, under the stress of the moment, *be able to grasp regulations and official procedures*. One example, an older lady with no kin, she describes as *lost in a world where people assumed that she had a social competence she had never possessed and could not learn.*

The responsibility for obtaining their rights lies with the free citizen who can choose to exit (remove their custom), vote or to complain to the unsatisfactory provider. Thus the per-ceived paternalism of the welfare state is reduced or removed. However, when entrance to the system depends on influencing those in authority positions who are operating in a cli-mate of increasing budget limitation and rationing, the social skill and status of the most vulnerable becomes an issue. The enabled citizen is an ideal whose reality may be quite limited, perhaps not only by age and health status but also by education and social class (Jones, 1998).

The argument that fund-holding GPs might 'cream skim' patients least likely to be expen-sive (Glennerster et al., 1994) is one aspect of this concern. Cochrane (1998) argues that far from being enabled by consumer status in the welfare market, there exists a reduced emphasis on accountability that has resulted in *passive consumers receiving what is best for them* according to the accountants who are the only experts who are not challenged. He cites William Waldegrave, whilst responsible for the creation of the Citizen's Charter, as stating that *democratic accountability was irrelevant to the operation of the local welfare state*. The quality of service, measurable above all by its economy, Cochrane argues, is the only politically correct standard applied and thus citizenship is devalued.

Older people's social rights

'Dis-welfare' for the older person in a climate of consumerism and individual competitive-ness may originate in misconceptions about the nature of community and family life in the 1990s. Mayo (1994) points out that the supportive community implied by Care in the Community is essentially a feminine phenomenon and the burden of caring has historically fallen to women. The economic necessity for women to work, failure of the benefits system to support working carers, increasing divorce and serial marriage, the geographical dispersal of families, and increasing numbers of the very old who have no surviving family, are cited as flaws in the concept of community care (Mayo, 1994; Jones, 1998).

Individuated citizenship, incorporating notions of articulate, assertive people consciously seeking their own self-interest in competition with others in their relations with the wel-fare state, it may be argued, is inherently discriminatory against the less competitively placed in society. The subordinate position of social rights, compared to political and civil rights, by virtue of their lack of legal enforceability (Dean, 1996), leaves those with the greatest dependency on the welfare state with the greatest need to compete effectively and be proactive in their own interests.

The rhetoric of freedom of the individual and responsive organisations, and the decentralisation of responsibility, through managerialisation, creation of NHS Trusts and devolved budgets, co-exist with tightening central control of overall public spending. Clarke and Newman (1998) describe the tensions between the *centrifugal and centripetal* forces at work, which distance the centre from rationing at the individual and local level, the responsibility of Trusts, managers or professionals, whilst ensuring that the rights of the consumer render decisions about provision more transparent and the budgetary imperative to ration becomes more insistent. Nettleton and Burrows (1998) discuss the individualisation process from the perspective of a late-modern culture of personal risk reduction, life-planning and self-development. They argue that there is an increasing requirement to make long-term life plans and lifestyle choices, and that this has in part come from political policies designed to de-emphasise state responsibility for individuals and to give simplistic digests of information such as league tables and audits to facilitate decision-making.

Choice becomes an imperative, and the choice of a healthy lifestyle, and therefore freedom from illness and dependency, is an external mark of good citizenship. They echo a point made by Dean (1996) that *when resources are rationed, those who exercise their 'rights' successfully may do so at the expense of others*. Nettleton and Burrows (1998) see *the marketisation of welfare* as inhibiting the ability of individuals to make altruistic choices and therefore to achieve a sense of citizenship.

Conclusion

The recurrent base note of this chapter has been conflicting policy values: altruism and self-interest, enablement and constraint, freedom of choice and control of choice available. Dean (1996) in his discussion of social rights concluded that social rights have been seen as *unavoidably dependent on and subordinate to the imperative of economic productivity*, even by left of centre thinkers. This all pervasive culture of materialism leaves the vulnerable older persons, and other disadvantaged groups in society, denied their social rights by virtue of the redefinition of citizenship in terms of competition. The emergent picture has been of older persons manipulated as economic counters between budget-holding institutions; enshrined as consumers but allowed to choose only through rationing professionals, and publicly defined as a burden on society.

Chapter 5

Intermediate care: implications for service users

Eileen Qubain

INTRODUCTION

This chapter will look at intermediate care, critically analyse the social and political factors which influence it, explore the way the service is organised, the impact on the service user and analyse how I identify networks and work effectively in complex situations.

The Kings Fund (2002) defines intermediate care as a:

short term intervention to preserve the independence of a person who might otherwise be forced to go into hospital or a nursing home. It is an active and intense way of helping those who have suffered from illness or injury to GET THEIR LIVES BACK. It includes a wide range of activities such as physiotherapy, speech and language therapy and practical support for everyday living.

Intermediate care

Steiner (2001, p433) describes intermediate care as a bridge between hospital and home for those who need a blend of medical and social support. A key component of intermediate care is rehabilitation, although the rehabilitation profession has resisted the word 'care' because it is suggestive of passivity and disempowerment (Steiner, 2001, p38). Contrary to this, intermediate care services are supportive rather than directive, they should be delivered in a way that is person centred, with support given in or near the person's home, or in a home-like setting. It is a bold move away from the usual model of care where the option of convalescence is seen as allowing time for the 'patient' to accept their increased weakness and disability.

Recent policy initiatives have placed *promoting independence* as a central theme in health and social care:

Social care should be given in ways that promote independence.

(Department of Health (DoH), 1998).

Intermediate care is a core element of the government's programme for improving services for older people, a concept that allows us to step outside safe and known methods of practice. It is seen as a radical change in the way health and social services operate. The philosophy and principles underlining Intermediate Care are driven by the National Health Service (NHS) Plan (DoH, 1999) and The National Services Framework for Older People (DoH, 2001) outlining the importance of care that is meaningful and relevant to people. Bound up in this is the single assessment process which should lead to coordinated and effective assessments converging across health and social boundaries, with one central point of access providing an assessment of need that is relevant, and which promotes older people's independence and dignity.

The commitment to person centred approaches

At the heart of health care there has always been the rhetoric of *Partnership* and *Inter-professional Working* is one of the terms expressed in government policy (DoH, 1998). This team work demands role clarification and agreements on how to move forward. Inevitably there may be disagreements and differences of opinion, but it seems to me that the ideology and principles behind these policies are nothing new; indeed most health and social care workers have always been committed to working in a way that is person centred and promotes independence. It is these values that attracted workers to their professions in the first place. Stevenson (2003, p20) described intermediate care as essentially old wine in new bottles. Back in 1968 Licht defined rehabilitation as *concern with the intrinsic worth and dignity of the individual*, whilst Sinclair and Dickinson (1998, p63) broaden the meaning as a

> *process aiming to restore personal autonomy in those aspects of daily living considered most relevant by patients or service users, and their family carers.*

This demonstrates that person centredness and work with family and carers has always been on the agenda. What is now different is that the government has articulated and legitimised these in guidance and statute, which compel the system to allow for this ethos to be practised at grass root levels, with support from managers.

The meaning of intermediate care

There are debates about the drive behind the concept of intermediate care. Kirby (2000, p8) suggests:

> *intermediate care is a new name designed to deal with an old problem – that of older patients staying in acute beds and causing winter crises.*

The powerful voice of older people who will have considerable influence at election time may be a significant factor in the government's promotion of the status of older people, but this may be only one part of a very complex issue.

Skerrett (2000, p64) sees social work as a social and political activity in which the welfare state is reflected. She takes this further by proposing that as social workers we cannot enable clients unless we are aware of the social context in which they live and how this is influenced by social policy. This view is supported by Brechin (2000, p25) who asserts that grasping the policy context of cases is vital in enabling practitioners to work effectively. In direct opposition Dunn (1985, p17) puts forward a picture of neglect of the political dimension by many nurses and related disciplines when she argues,

> *politics is for others. Politics is a deviant activity in which no self-respecting professional should indulge.*

It is important to look at the history of British social policy and grapple with this 'deviancy', acknowledging that

> *social work is the interaction between people and their environment.*

> (Banks, 1995, p63).

With the introduction of the Beveridge Report (1942) came the promise of collective protection against the ills of want, unemployment, disease, squalor and ignorance (Adams, 2002, p46). This welfare emphasis, which was to be universally available, was a distinct move away from the individualistic philosophy dominant in pre-war years based on a premise of the 'deserving and undeserving'. During the Conservative governments of Thatcher and Major, there was a return to free market capitalism, which supports an individualistic approach where the strong survive. This was very much influenced by Hayek who believed the concept of society to be a myth, a statement echoed by Margaret Thatcher, who felt that personal freedom should not be eroded by the state in terms of taxes or collective responsibility.

The state as care provider

Since Labour's rise to power in 1997, Blair has attempted to establish a new consensus around issues such as welfare, employment and citizenship citing (1998) *equal value, opportunity for all, responsibility and obligation* as key themes in the Third Way. In his recent Labour Party conference speech, Blair (2004) refers to a move away from the traditional welfare state and introduces a vision of an *opportunity society* where the individual has both rights and responsibilities. He identifies the central values of his new direction to be equity, solidarity and a society of mutual obligation. Interwoven in rhetoric about the Third Way there is a recurrent theme in references to *responsibility, obligation, contracts and reciprocity* with an underlying ambition to *break the mould of the old passive benefits system* (DSS, 1998 p24). Similarly, the Community Care Minister Stephen Ladyman (2004, p44) criticises models of social care provision which *hold people in a culture of dependency*, citing choice, diversity and person centredness as tenets of his 'bottom up' vision for the future of social care.

In this vein the State is seen as an agency that informs and guides people to make wise decisions about their health, diet, education and employment, fostering and formulating personal projects whilst instilling a sense of mutuality and drive towards the common good. Jordan (2000, p49) argues that there needs to be a presence and balance between individualism and collectivism for ethical social work practice, and it would seem that in his Third Way, Blair is attempting to balance these two elements. Achieving this balance is no easy feat and looking behind the rhetoric are shades of a return to 'deserving and undeserving'. Jordan (2000, p13) paints a powerful picture of the safety nets constructed by the Beveridge reforms being replaced with a trampoline to 'bounce' people out of the benefits system into independence. But what happens to those who cannot bounce? Intermediate care, with a focus on rehabilitation, could be seen as an instrument to help people bounce out of dependency and as such it is given prominence and funding in health and social care.

But behind the door of this rhetoric there are major factors knocking hard on the government's agenda, which cannot be ignored. There is the tremendous influence of an ageing society, where between 1995 and 2025 the number of people over the age of 80 in England is set to increase by almost half, and the number of people over 90 will double (DoH, 2001). This, coupled with the economic factors, and the cost of long-term care provision, is significant and the government has had to look at ways of managing this.

The value of intermediate care

I would argue that intermediate care is a robust vehicle to support and empower people, but its effectiveness is dependent on its definition and application. The question is:

- Is the endeavour and bedrock of intermediate care, reinforced by the National Services Framework for Older People (DoH, 2001), to motivate, empower and promote self-esteem, or is it a tool for bed management?

In my locality we have a wealth of intermediate care service, which provides intensive short-term support, and sees service users through a critical period by promoting independence and rehabilitation opportunity. These services can be located in a community unit, within a residential or nursing home setting, or within a person's own home, and we consider that we are fairly wealthy in terms of the options available to us in our area. The impact of intermediate care within our wider hospital based team has been a powerful one and there have been good inter-disciplinary links developed over time. These have been extended and strengthened by the vehicle of intermediate care in which a high level of partnership is required. It has given a clearer definition of multi-disciplinary working and improved understanding of the roles and values each team member has. We share not only a budget, but also expertise, knowledge, skills, and responsibility, which has forced us to constantly articulate and re-shape our shared aims and visions in each individual piece of work. It has also provided a forum for learning from each other, sharing experiences and disappointments, evaluating our successes or lack of it, and for our practices to suit the individual. We have learned that spending time together is key to improving our sense of belonging to the team.

We have experienced tensions and disagreements prompted by extreme pressure and limited resources, but by working more closely together, we have found ways of resolving these. There are times when we begin to revert to the bitter question of whether this is a 'medical' or a 'social' problem, and time and energy is wasted on debating this. In truth, it is hard to unpick the threads and separate the two. Being in close proximity is crucial, and having regular meetings and reviews helps our steps to be coordinated, and makes working together infinitely easier. In the future I believe that these foundations could and must be taken further with opportunities for joint training, sharing away-days to look at specific health and social care issues, and reminding and updating our vision of what our service is.

The people who are referred to our service need support to 'get their lives back' when it feels as if part of it has been stolen by acute illness, disability, or an exacerbation of their chronic condition. On the whole, there is scope for incredible flexibility, and we look at a way forward together within the confines of the limitations placed on us by the harsh reality of eligibility criteria, stretched services and financial pressure. Where there have been 'clashes' we have worked hard at talking things through in a way that is both respectful and upholds the bonds we have worked so hard to develop. There is too much to lose, both for us as a team and for the people with whom we work, to jeopardise these relationships which determine the success or failure of our service. Hudson (1991, p78) states:

> *It is clear that collaboration in social welfare has no qualities of spontaneous growth or self-perpetuation. Progress will only stem from the most vigorous commitments.*

The rationale of intermediate care

As a social worker I find the concepts and rationale behind the ideas of intermediate care to be liberating both for the person and the team involved. I believe it invites us to adopt a social model of care, rather than slavery to traditional and narrow confines inherent in a medical model. Ryan and Thomas (1987, p27) suggest, *Medical model thinking tends to support the status quo.* Intermediate care heartily dispels the myth that patients should be passive recipients of care. It has given control and power back to the person, making the patients 'director of their own care', as well as giving to nurses and other team members what Binnie and Titchen (1999) describe as *Freedom to Practise*. It questions the role of 'consultant' as the only expert, underlines the idea of client expertise in themselves, as well as elevating and nurturing the status of the team. This idea of professional autonomy pulls us together, and invites us to practise in a way that suits the person and the context in which they live, rather than the organisation for which we work. I feel that our values and philosophies, now shaped and underpinned by intermediate care, should no longer be different. There is not the same struggle over finances and responsibility, although this remains a potentially explosive area. We have learned mutual respect for the different constraints of each discipline involved. We have struggled together over 'rights versus risks' issues in looking at promoting independence, balanced with safety. We have together shaped the way our team has evolved and because of tight timescales, there has been imperative for good and frequent communication.

Fennell et al. (1988, p17) alludes to *unwarranted application of negative stereotypes to older people*. There has been a tendency for older people to be dismissed and have their humanity denied as they are often presented as useless and a burden. In countering this Phillipson (1989, p205) introduces *interdependency* which he claims:

> *Provides recognition of help older people need from us, as well as rewards to be gained from giving this help. It also reminds us of skills possessed by older people and the resources these might provide for activities and campaigns within the community.*

Secker et al. (2003, p386) identifies reciprocity as a main theme emerging in literature about independence and highlight the importance of creating and maximising opportunities for older people to engage in reciprocal networks of support. This is something that intermediate care can offer with opportunities to enable people to step back into their place and life in the community where they have a valuable contribution to make, if this is what they wish to do. An example of this has been working with someone who wanted very much to increase her mobility so that she could attend church on Sundays; another wanted to resume his place as chairperson for the Severn Valley Railway Association. Cresswell (1996, p180) asks

> *What is social work if it is not the interlinking of systems, and the ways of working with them? Networking is essential to execute the principles of community care.*

Building on strengths

In intermediate care the personal resources a service user has at their disposal is as crucial as the 'professional' networks we work within. These personal networks should act as a guide in looking at what wider support is needed and available. Middleton (1994, p79) states that assessments should start with the hopes and aspirations of users and carers, rather than looking outside for answers, and dwelling on deficits and difficulties. Intermediate care with its emphasis on person-centred care should build on the individual's strengths and coping strategies, rather than undermining them. Sometimes through critical life events the networks people have are weakened, and intermediate care has a role in helping to strengthen them, by offering support, practical advice and assistance. Research has highlighted the importance of building on family cohesion and their internal organisation (Dale, 1996, p31) and there are times when we have jumped in too quickly and offered support that does not fit in with the person's own network or system. Similarly, there have been times when we have failed to realise the struggle of family and carers and have assumed that they are able and prepared to continue caring, when it comes to light that this is not the case. These are errors made when we fail to adequately listen to people, and when the pressures of moving things on leads to us losing sight of the person and their carers.

Research shows (Green, 1996, p382) that older people are less likely than other patients to be involved in joint decision-making with health professionals, and some studies done find that they are not consulted at all (Minichiello, 2000, p253). Paterson (2001, p574) contends that the culture of the *practitioner as expert* is deep-rooted and that accepting lay knowledge as being of equal value raises fundamental challenges for the way in which practitioners view themselves. The National Services Framework tackles this issue by stating a directive that age discrimination is rooted out, and that care should be person centred. Intermediate care goes a long way to addressing the problem of 'people being done to' and demands that choice and decision-making are handed back to the person wherever possible. DoH (2001) acknowledges that there must be a *major shift in culture and attitude....if disabled people and their families are to be engaged as experts*. In our area all notes are left at the service user's home, and they have access to read and add any information or reflections they have. This is a shared record of the aims and support in place to achieve these, with the ultimate ownership being with the service user. This has had an impact on service users, many of whom are puzzled and surprised that they can access their notes, and contribute to them. This does not eradicate hidden agendas altogether but goes a considerable way to inclusion and honest communication. Steiner (2001, p434) identifies that the potential of intermediate care is uniting professionals in their efforts to listen to older patients, elicit patients' individual goals and provide the services that will empower older people to come as close to meeting these goals as is possible. This firmly places the 'patient' at the centre of any work done and so building a framework of support around the patients' networks and resources should be the natural starting point. Smale et al. (1993, p116) recognise that

people are experts in themselves, their situations, relationships and needs.

The core of intermediate care

A central feature of intermediate care is that it acknowledges the links between the functional view of 'rehabilitation' and 'existential concerns' such as 'personal identity' and 'loss of self', often eroded through chronic ill health. There is a tendency to equate quality of life with functional ability only, and look at activities of daily living and assess only practicalities of 'self care' skills. A majority of our service users are older people and Steiner (2001, p 434) identifies that for older people it is quality of life, and not physical function, which is central, and it must be recognised that independence means something very different to each one of us.

Corbett (1989, p153) states:

Real independence is nothing to do with cooking, cleaning, and dressing oneself. If you ask me what is my experience of being independent, I would not automatically think about self help skills but of being able to use my imagination to create fantasy, of enjoying music and drama, of relishing sensual pleasure and absorbing the natural life around me.

Rehabilitation needs to 'be relevant' and meaningful to people and it should enable us to see what works for one person in the 'healing process' does not necessarily work for another. Geelen and Soons (1996, pp69–77) refer to information being given to patients in a way that fits into their world and experience, acknowledging that metaphorical images intermeshed with areas of interest of the person can prove useful and powerful. They site an example of a retired car mechanic with arthritis in his knee joints being given an explanation of his condition in which there is comparison made with poor shock absorbers in a car. In order to be able to make these links and capitalise on the resources people have within them, time has to be invested in getting to know and understand the person, what matters to them, what they want to achieve and what motivates them. For some of the service users we have worked with they have indicated what really matters to them is getting out to the hairdressers or the bookmakers, rather than being able to stand in the kitchen and cook a meal. For some this is how life quality is measured, and indeed why should we impose our standards and ideals on another person, who has their own wealth of knowledge and their own pattern of life which they value and hold dear? Having this goal gives motivation and the will to participate in the rehabilitation process and intermediate care gives us the opportunity to be creative and flexible in accommodating need as far as we are able.

However, over the time that intermediate care has developed in our area, the pressures of speedy hospital discharges have gathered momentum, and with the implementation of the Community Care (Delayed Discharges) Act 2003 there is an increased imperative to move people on. On personal reflection, I feel that there is less opportunity to work with existential concerns and that the drive is now to concentrate on the functional abilities of people to 'bounce them out' of an over-stretched system. There remain windows for looking beyond this, but this appears to be dependent on the will, motivation and drive of the different intermediate care resources and the staff who manage them. This highlights the need for excellent multi-disciplinary work with a shared vision and culture. Without this, the opportunities inherent in intermediate care are lost, and it is at serious risk of becoming *an antidote for the bed blocking crisis* (Wade and Lees, 2002, p8).

The range of intermediate care services locally provides a plethora of choice and, if used correctly, we have countless examples of people who have benefited greatly from support in these different circumstances. However, there are also examples when people are passed from one service to the other. One service user described feeling like a 'package' being passed around. In looking at staffing changes in the NHS Williams (1992, p153) asserts that there is *no longer cradle to grave, but from pillar to post*. With the introduction of different pockets of intermediate care services, this is a real issue for many older, vulnerable and bewildered service users who are passed from one resource to another. Biggs (1993, p153) states that service users often have considerable experience of relying on services that are organised around priorities other than their own, and this appears to be an increasing danger in intermediate care. This makes a nonsense of the idea of a 'seamless service' which is identified as an aim in service provision, and begs the question, for whose benefit are these services instituted?

Who can benefit from intermediate care?

There is also a drive towards ensuring that only the 'right type of person', who presents as being motivated, cooperative and able to benefit from what is on offer, receives intermediate care, rationing the stretched resources to ensure the most effective use of service. I understand that there is not a bottomless pot of money and that there needs to be some rationing. However, I also feel that behind this there are shades of the deserving and undeserving, with vulnerable people almost having to prove their worth in the rehabilitation arena, or have someone who will argue their case for them if they are unable. If they cannot be seen to 'fit into' what services are on offer, then people do not have those choices or opportunities. In this 'value for money culture', where there are targets to meet and beds to empty, there is decreasing drive to look at the emotional needs bound up in rehabilitation, and lost opportunities in a system whose rhetoric boasts helping people to get their lives back.

The effect on carers

Another major issue is the impact that intermediate care can have on carers. With the emphasis on providing support outside of the setting of the acute sector, and wherever possible within a person's own home, there is a danger that carers', needs can be overlooked in the assessment process. The Carers Recognition and Services Act 1995 has signalled the fact that carers should no longer be *the Cinderellas of social policy* (Twigg and Atkin, 1994, p80), but there remains a tremendous pressure and expectation on carers to be a key part of the process, when this may not be what the carer wants. Traditionally, when the cared for person has been admitted into hospital this is a time for the carer to have a break from the caring role. Intermediate care has the potential to work with carers in a positive way by looking at support networks that may help them in their role, and identify resources available to carers in their own right. It can allow the opportunity for a carer's assessment to be done away from the frenzy of a hospital admission where many carers decline an assessment of their own needs. This can lead to emotional help, as well as some practical assistance and guidance. I have been able to do some carer's assessments within intermediate care which has opened up all sorts of support and has given the carer a wider access to the multi-disciplinary team in addressing their concerns and worries. Within the acute setting this is not always possible.

Conclusion

On balance, my observation and experience of intermediate care has been positive, with people being freed from making permanent and life-changing decisions at a time of great crisis. The majority of cases referred to the intermediate care team are complex, and behind the initial contact reason, there are often many other chronic medical problems and underlying issues, which complicate the road to recovery. I have witnessed people regaining their confidence, dignity and place in their community where intermediate care has allowed flexibility in goal planning. As a team we have the opportunity to look at wider issues of discrimination, power and disadvantage, an area I feel that social workers are particularly tuned into. Thompson (1993, p10) asserts that a social work practice that does not take account of oppression and discrimination cannot be seen as good practice.

In this area I feel that we have something to offer our health colleagues as these issues are not discussed as widely in their training structures, and yet they are a foundation of social work training. Using the strengths and expertise of different team members assists in complex cases where there is a need for multiple skills, and different approaches to achieve a positive outcome. In cases where people have not benefited as they should, or have not had access to the services they should have, it seems mostly to have been the result of a loss of shared vision and purpose within the multi-disciplinary team. This is often caused by a breakdown in communication and an overriding pressure to move people on.

Critical analysis of work and self is crucial in working within an anti-oppressive framework. Hopson (1981, p154) suggests

> *we are unable to help others if we do not know ourselves, our own strengths and weaknesses.*

As a team, acknowledging and working with these issues is imperative in developing true partnership. Working in a climate of collaboration, cooperation and clear communication makes work more fulfilling and therefore staff morale increases, which cascades down to the service user. Nolan and his colleagues (Nolan, 1997; Davies et al., 1999; Nolan et al., 2001) suggest that staff are unlikely to be able to create an environment in which an older person feels significant, and that they matter, if they themselves do not feel valued. As a team we have noted how respect and value are infectious, and feedback from service users indicate that they do feel valued and listened to, and this in turn increases the possibility for positive recovery. We feel that the quality of the service we provide is heavily dependent on the quality of the relationships we develop.

Steiner (2001, p434) refers to controversy around intermediate care and asserts that it is both a puzzle and a challenge. In managing this, tools such as theory, legislation, codes of practice, supervision and the opportunity for informal discussion with colleagues help me deal with difficulties presented. Casement (1985, p136) suggests that developing an *internal supervisor* allows one to stand outside one's self to monitor the complex processes and dynamics entailed in work. This is especially true in intermediate care where it is easy to get driven along, when sometimes the right thing to do is to 'slow things down' to allow us as a team to look at the whole picture. I hope that we can build on the positive foundation we have for intermediate care in our area and work with

the challenge to move beyond the rhetoric to make person centred care visible.

(Nolan, 2000, p49)

Chapter 6

Do Direct Payments offer people with learning disabilities greater choice and control?

Jonathan Monk

INTRODUCTION

A core value of social work practice is to promote people's rights to choice and assist them to increase control of and improve the quality of their lives. Direct Payments are seen as a major tool to support independent living and as a means of empowering users to have enhanced choice, freedom and control over their own lives (Hasler et al., 1999).

This chapter will analyse the political and social context in which Direct Payments were introduced and which influence the current implementation and delivery of the service. The chapter will then go on to evaluate the implementation of Direct Payments on both a micro and macro level, to consider the impact on the individual and also for social work practice and social welfare provision for people with learning disabilities, balancing the rhetoric with the realities in practice. There will be a critical examination of the effectiveness of the use of Direct Payments to support people with learning disabilities to increase their levels of choice and control over their daily lives. The paper will then apply models of good practice and set out examples of tools to illustrate how Direct Payments can assist people with learning disabilities to exercise greater choice and control in the decisions that impact on their lives in order to extend their opportunities for independent living.

The social and political context of direct payments

The Community Care (Direct Payments) Act 1996 gave local authorities the power to make financial payments to people eligible for community care support in order to purchase their own support services as an alternative to receiving services that were purchased or provided by the local authority. This power extended only to adults below the age of 65. However, new regulations in February 2000 rectified this age inequality and the power to make Direct Payments was eventually extended to older people, under the Labour government.

The law was amended again with the implementation of the Health and Social Care Act 2001 and the associated Community Care, Services for Carers and Children's Services

(Direct Payments) Regulations 2003. This extended Direct Payments to carers (including young carers) who are entitled to receive services under the Carers and Disabled Children Act 2000 and to people with parental responsibility for a child.

Whilst the 1996 Act provided a discretionary power to local authorities to make Direct Payments, this was not mandatory and there was no guarantee of local availability. However, under the 2003 Regulations, essentially it is set out that local authorities now have a *duty* to make Direct Payments to all individuals who are assessed as being eligible for community care support (with the exception of permanent residential care) and who consent to receiving this support in the form of a Direct Payment (Dow, 2004, p20).

Prior to the 1996 Act, under the National Assistance Act, there was a specific prohibition against local authorities making cash payments in lieu of providing community care services. However, as a result of pressure from organisations of disabled people, some local authorities gave financial grants to voluntary organisations to administer third party 'indirect payments' arrangements. Spandler (2004, p88) suggests that the emergence of Direct Payments was underpinned by the philosophy of independent living, the social model of disability and criticism of the medical model. The social model of disability argues that it is not the person's impairment that limits their ability to fully participate in society and to exercise control over their rights and choices, but the organisation of society itself, and in this case, the organisation of welfare services, which cause the disability and disadvantage (Stainton, 2002, p752). To this end, the disability movement argued that in order to achieve independent/integrated living, emphasis had to be placed on *securing the resources with which disabled people might manage their own affairs* (Priestley, 1999, p99). Therefore, the philosophy and eventual implementation of Direct Payments represented a significant move towards independent living for many people.

The development and introduction of Direct Payments initially received cautious support from the serving Conservative government. Pearson (2000, p461) suggests that the government were concerned with *cost efficiency and accountability of public spending*, whilst there were also uncertainties of the potential demand for the scheme.

However, the notion of Direct Payments reflected contemporary ideologies of self help and individualism in response to government concerns about 'welfare dependency' (Means et al., 2003). This agenda converged with the disability movements' growing criticism of inadequate, inflexible and insensitive service provision (Spandler, 2004, p189). Alongside this, Direct Payments reflected the drive to introduce market forces and managerialism into welfare services, whereby users became part of the 'mixed economy' of care as employers of personal assistants. This was further consolidated by Direct Payments users being seen as consumers with the power to commission services from a range of private and independent providers. The growing voluntary sector also played a key role in the mixed economy through the establishment of independent Direct Payments support schemes. Priestley (1999, p12) argues that such an increase in the purchasing power of individual disabled people demonstrates classical free market thinking and stimulates individual choice, freedom and empowerment: all fundamental components of the philosophy of Direct Payments. However, the extent that free market thinking is achieved through Direct Payments is arguable, as essentially the scheme is still publicly funded. Within this model, user choices and freedoms are dependent on the existence of public welfare services, through the application of ever-restrictive definitions of needs assessment based on eligibility criteria implemented by the local authority. In this context, powers and choices for the user as a consumer are also dependent on a thriving independent and private sector to act as a service provider, alongside the availability of personal assistants.

Implications of Direct Payments

There are implications for the user's ability to compete within the quasi-market when recruiting personal assistants and attracting suitably skilled workers, whereby:

> *many Direct Payment users had experienced difficulty in recruiting suitable staff...many disabled people attributed this to the low rates of pay they could offer, compared to the pay offered by care agencies and social services departments.*

> (Glendinning et al., 2000, p206)

Therefore, the notion of users as consumers in a market place where they can exercise free choice is misleading. Essentially, the extent to which choice can be exercised is dependent on the resources and the power of the consumer; this in itself is dependent on the user's eligibility for community care support, which is ultimately defined by the local authority (Banks, 1995, p103).

Spandler (2004, p190) argues that the introduction of Direct Payments demonstrates a *complex confluence* of Conservative government and disability movement ideologies, demands and priorities. This agenda is further represented in New Labour's development of a 'Third Way' programme for social care which:

> *should be provided for people in a way that supports their independence and respects their dignity.*

> (DOH, 1998, cited in Jordan, 2001, p528)

New Labour's overwhelming support for Direct Payments represented this model's view of people as *consumer citizens* whereby users could expect quality, person centred and individualised packages of support based on their choices, freedoms and self-direction. However, alongside these opportunities to gain increased choice and control, New Labour place increased emphasis on responsibility, accountability, participation and obligation (Jordan, 2001, p529). The ideological concepts of a Third Way whereby *opportunity and responsibility going together* (Blair, 1997, cited in Jordan, 2001, p530) to promote user choice and control sits very comfortably with the philosophy and language of Direct Payments. Indeed, Direct Payments should certainly be perceived as a tool to promote the extension of disabled people's social rights, particularly in relation to the duty to make Direct Payments to eligible people. Moreover, the introduction of market principles between disabled people and their personal assistants, and the contractual obligations this involves, should instil the care dynamic with rights protected by contract and employ-ment law (Ungerson, 1997, p151). However, such a framework of rights, responsibilities and obligations also includes notions of capacity and consent. This has significant implica-tions for Direct Payments practice with people with learning disabilities and will be discussed later in this chapter.

Valuing people

As part of this agenda for the modernisation of welfare services, *Valuing People: A New Strategy for Learning Disability for the 21st Century* was published in March 2001. The *Valuing People* White Paper declared that people with learning disabilities lack independence and have little choice and control in all aspects of their lives whilst their views are rarely taken into consideration. *Valuing People* is explicit in its aims and sets out four key objectives. Firstly, that people with learning disabilities should have enforceable civil and legal rights in order to ensure their full protection within law and to drive out discrimination and oppression. Secondly, that the aim of services for people with learning disabilities is to promote independence. Thirdly, that people with learning disabilities should be empowered to express preferences and make choices in all aspects of daily living. Finally, the strategy aims to reduce exclusion for people with learning disabilities by ensuring that people should be able to access mainstream services and be fully included in their local community.

Valuing People was generally welcomed for its commitment to the rights of people with learning disabilities and emphasis on person-centred approaches and partnership working (Means et al., 2003, p93). At the heart of the White Paper's recommendations was the extension and development of Direct Payments for people with learning disabilities as a key action for improving a person's choice and control over their lives. It is in this context that Direct Payments are viewed as:

> *facilitating people to live in the ways that they choose rather than being given services to match perceived assumptions about what is needed and how individuals should live.*
>
> (Spandler, 2004, p192)

The introduction of direct payments and effectiveness of implementation

The implementation of Direct Payments has the capacity to fundamentally change the organisation and delivery of community care service provision in the UK. Indeed, Holman (1999, p3) argues that for people with learning disabilities, Direct Payments are the *most empowering* means of shifting power and resources to enable users to have choice in their own support arrangements and to ultimately take control over their lives.

Direct Payments can enable users to purchase a wider range of flexible support, resulting in:

- greater continuity of care;
- enhanced emotional and psychological wellbeing;
- increased opportunities to participate in social, community and family life;
- greater control;
- and an enhanced quality of life (Glendinning et al., 2000, p201).

Spandler (2004, p192) suggests that these claims are *extremely compelling* and that they appear to be mirrored by people's actual experience of using Direct Payments, whereby high user satisfaction is reported, particularly in relation to the opportunity to exercise choice, control and flexibility over support arrangements (see, for example McMullen (2003)).

Criticisms and concerns

However, the implementation of Direct Payments has resulted in some criticism and concerns about the scheme. The recent 2003 Direct Payments Regulations can be described as being 'loose' and imprecise. This has therefore resulted in variable and inconsistent interpretation of the guidance that has influenced local implementation. Indeed, Pearson (2000, p467) argues that the choice and flexibility of the Direct Payments package can engender maximum user control but it is this factor that varies so greatly between each local authority. This suggests a 'postcode lottery' of disadvantage for those people wanting to take greater control over their own support arrangements but who live in what can be deemed as 'less progressive' local authorities.

Within Direct Payments discourse, there has also been concern that the

> *overwhelming justification for these types of funding schemes appears to be cost savings to the system.*

> (National Research Union, 2000, cited in Spandler, 2004, p194)

Indeed, it is argued that any dominance of cost efficiency, particularly that results in prescriptive attempts to 'police' the use of Direct Payments, significantly weakens the consumer power of the user and limits the scope for choice and control (Spandler, 2004 p197). This also reflects the consumer citizen dynamic of the Third Way, whereby the user has choices and freedoms as a consumer but conversely has responsibilities and obligations as a citizen to account for their spending and use of the Direct Payment.

In relation to Direct Payments being viewed as an initiative that is overwhelmingly concerned with cost savings, under the 1996 Act local authorities had the discretion to take into account the principles of 'Best Value' in whether to make Direct Payments, whereby the payment had to be *at least as cost effective as the services which it would otherwise arrange* (paragraph 25 of the 1996 Act guidance). However, within the 2003 regulations, there is no longer any reference to Best Value. Therefore, it would appear that the duty to make Direct Payments applies irrespective of the cost of arranging alternative services. This has significant implications for the levels of independence and options for community living available for people using Direct Payments in that the legislation requires that the amount of Direct Payment must be equivalent to the local authority's estimate of the reasonable cost of securing the provision of the relevant service (Dow, 2004, p2). Under this principle, taking into consideration the increasing costs of securing residential care arrangements for people with learning disabilities and the eligibility for Independent Living Fund and potential to access Supporting People and Health funding, the user has far greater choice and flexibility of options to remain living in the community or to move into independent living arrangements. However, the local authority is not obliged to make Direct Payments to fund the particular costs associated with the individual's preferred way of securing the service if the costs exceed the local authority's estimate of the reasonable cost of securing an equivalent, thus placing limitations on user choice, control and powers as a consumer citizen.

The flexibilities associated with Direct Payments have also raised concerns in relation to resource implications for local authorities. Pearson (2000, p466) suggests that a high demand for Direct Payments instead of traditional social care services will have commissioning and staffing implications that could result in double funding or loss of the service, such as traditional day opportunities and respite short break facilities.

There are also concerns arising from the specific effects of the marketisation of social care, such as:

- poor working conditions;

- low pay;

- health and safety considerations;

- difficulties with recruitment of personal assistants;

- lack of training opportunities for personal assistants;

- and the lack of responsive and quality service providers (Spandler, 2004, p197).

Spandler (ibid., p188) argues that another 'reactionary' view of Direct Payments stems from a desire to discharge responsibility for so-called 'difficult' service users or where Direct Payments are seen as a 'last resort' where an alternative satisfactory response cannot be found to meet a person's needs. There are also issues of equity, with many professionals perceiving Direct Payments as a 'Rolls Royce' option (Gramlich et al., 2002, p10). Such views do not represent true opportunities for empowerment and do not reflect the principles of user choice and control that should be fundamental within good Direct Payments practice and the *Valuing People* White Paper. Indeed, the regulations are explicit that Direct Payments should not be a 'last resort' or 'optional extra'; Direct Payments should be a core option within mainstream community care services (ibid., p17).

Take up of Direct Payments

However, recent findings concerning the implementation of Direct Payments highlight that there is a long way to go before the scheme becomes part of mainstream social care provision. Unity Sale and Leason (2004, p29) state that despite the known advantages of using Direct Payments, the take up has been relatively low with

only a very small number of people with learning disabilities using Direct Payments.

To support these findings, the Delivery and Improvement Statements for local authorities in 2003 reported that only 1,337 people with a learning disability were using Direct Payments in England; from a total 12,585 Direct Payments recipients (Commission for Social Care Inspection, 2004, p8). If compared to the number of people with learning disabilities who access community care services, this number is negligible. In Worcestershire less than one per cent of the total number of people with learning disabilities who access community care services has received and uses Direct Payments.

What are the reasons for low take up of direct payments amongst people with learning difficulties?

People with learning disabilities have been included in the Direct Payments regulations from the 1996 Act. However, Holman (1999, p2) argues that their inclusion was

> *a last minute addition and consequently neither the legislation nor accompanying guidance fully addresses their needs and support systems.*

Indeed, whilst the Act provided, in theory, opportunities for people with learning disabilities to have greater choice, independence and control over their lives, the reality was very different.

The evidence from the first few years of the introduction and implementation of Direct Payments was 'so dismal' concerning the take up and use amongst people with learning disabilities that the Department of Health was moved to commission a research project into the low take up and would subsequently review the guidance (Hasler, 2003, p10). The *Funding Freedom* Report (2000, cited in Hasler, 2003, p10) by the Values into Action voluntary organisation conveyed that the barriers to Direct Payments for people with learning disabilities were:

- problems within legislation and guidance;

- local authority procedures and policy;

- attitudes of professionals;

- lack of appropriate support systems;

- lack of suitable, accessible information;

- assumptions around the assessment of consent;

- over-simplistic application of the 'ability to manage' criteria contained in the guidance.

The 1996 legislation stated that potential users must consent to receiving a Direct Payment, and the associated guidance affirmed that they should be *willing and able* to manage it. In response to this criteria, many people with learning disabilities were perceived as being ineligible to access Direct Payments. In addition to this and the discretionary power to make Direct Payments, as contained in the 1996 Act, some local authorities developed blanket policies that specifically excluded people with learning disabilities from receiving Direct Payments. However, the duty to make Direct Payments under the 2003 regulations and the increased emphasis on the ability to manage with whatever support is required was thought to address this disadvantage and inequality of provision (Ladyman, 2004, cited in DoH, 2004, piv).

Whilst this may address some of the policy issues that influence the take up of Direct Payments for people with learning disabilities, there are many other factors that act as barriers. Spandler (2004, p188) suggests that inadequate local authority responses with an over-reliance on traditional and established ways of working is a significant factor alongside professional resistance based on fear of change; risk aversion; paternalism; and reluctance to give up control and power. Clarke and Spafford (2002, p254) argue that there remains a tendency among professionals to define people with disabilities in relation to medical diagnosis or some other individual pathology such as 'vulnerability', 'dependency' or 'unable'. This 'deficit' approach neglects to take into account the capacities of the individual, which can often be used to exclude the person from decision-making and planning. As part of this, it is clear that professionals are concerned with the tensions that exist between protecting vulnerable people and empowering users to take risks, make choices and have greater control over their daily lives; for example, concerns that the arrangements made by the user will not be adequate to meet their needs or that personal assistants may financially abuse or exploit the individual.

Concerns also exist regarding the perceived bureaucracy, paperwork and administrative demands of using Direct Payments amongst professionals, service users and carers. In relation to this, there is much confusion about what Direct Payments actually involve for the service user, carers or supporters and for the professionals themselves (D'Ahoville et al., 2000, cited in Gramlich et al., 2002, p11).

Problems with information and communication

In a recent CSCI report (2004, p15), the lack of appropriate and accessible information was repeatedly raised as a barrier to take up. This lack of adequate information and awareness exists on many levels and has far reaching implications. The fundamental principle is that people with learning disabilities can exercise very little control over their lives and the services they use if they are not aware that they have choices and do not have information about what choices are available to them. Gramlich et al. (2002, p51) report that from the research they conducted into the provision of Direct Payments information for people with learning disabilities, people first heard about Direct Payments in one of three ways:

● from their social worker (but only if there had been a crisis);

● from other families or friends who were using Direct Payments;

● and from groups they belonged to such as the local People First group.

It is clear that information about Direct Payments is not reaching the people who need it and when information is provided, it can have the perverse effect of dissuading people from using the scheme, as it is often presented in such a way that discourages people from wanting to use Direct Payments or will mislead them into thinking that they would not be able to manage (CSCI, 2004, p15).

Social workers, service providers and other professionals are also often unclear and ill-informed about Direct Payments (Holman, 1999, p2). There is a feeling that they do not fully understand the purpose and philosophy of Direct Payments or of their potential for many of the people they work with (CSCI, 2004, p16). Much confusion has also come from the recently introduced 'Direct Payment' scheme from the Department of Work and Pensions, in relation to the payment of welfare benefits.

Policy responses from local authorities have also been perceived as a significant barrier to the growth of the scheme. Some local authorities appear to be over-prescriptive about how Direct Payments can be used, thus removing the flexibility, choice and control which the payments were intended to promote. Holman (1999, p2) suggests that some local authorities were also reluctant to change the pattern of existing service provision, particularly in relation to authorities with block contracts with providers and investments in the structures and staffing of existing services, such as day centres and residential units. It is also argued that Direct Payments are *perceived as a threat to a healthy and vibrant* public and independent sector (Spandler, 2004, p195).

The availability of person centred support systems has also found to be 'patchy' and inadequate within some local authorities (CSCI, 2004, p5). Hasler (2003, p11) states that lack of suitable support, particularly for people with learning disabilities, is a fundamental problem in instilling confidence to pro-actively use Direct Payments amongst users, carers and professionals. She argues that the lack of individualised and tailored support systems for people with learning disabilities introduces a *vicious circle* whereby *lack of support service leads to lack of referrals, lack of numbers leads to lack of support*. Hence, whilst numbers remain low, it is hard to justify the case for specialised support services.

Improving access to Direct Payments for people with learning disabilities

Given that the evidence in favour of Direct Payments has been explored throughout this study and that the barriers discussed exist, the question is what can be done to improve the access to Direct Payments for people with learning disabilities as a means of *promoting independence and freedom of choice* (Ladyman, 2003, cited in McMullen, 2003, p3).

To further consolidate the Labour government's commitment to using Direct Payments to promote independence and freedom of choice for people needing care and support, in June 2004 Health Minister Dr Stephen Ladyman allocated £4.5 million to 44 charities to establish and boost projects to encourage people to take up Direct Payments (Social Services Parliamentary Monitor, 2004, p17). Through partnership working with local authorities, voluntary organisations were allocated funding to establish schemes and initiatives to raise awareness of Direct Payments and improve accessibility to reflect

> *how valuable Direct Payments are and how important it is for the Government to ensure that people are able to exercise much more control and choice in their lives.*

> (ibid.)

It is interesting to note the emphasis on the voluntary sector taking a lead role in the establishment of such initiatives and the bidding process for funding from the Department of Health Direct Payment Development Fund.

Priestley (1999, p113), in his analysis of the marketisation of social care, argues that the promotion of market economics in social welfare is *characterised by an ideological attachment to individual freedom...and choice*. Many of the Development Fund Projects have been established by user-led organisations whereby users sit on the board of trustees and have direct involvement in the organisation and delivery of the service, thus providing real opportunities to promote choice, control and independence. It is important to note that many disabled people have been as critical of voluntary organisations 'for' disabled people as they have been of the inflexible and disabling service provision within the public and private sectors (ibid. p117). In this context, the distinction between organisations of disabled people and organisations for disabled people is important, with the first being an *increasingly potent force* for participation, changing professional practice and social attitudes (Oliver and Sapey, 1999, p169). It could be argued that this will have an influence on the success of the Development Fund Projects and the effectiveness of promoting Direct Payments as a means of empowering people to exercise more choice and control over their own support arrangements, through the introduction of peer support and mentoring schemes; increased user involvement in Direct Payments training for professionals; and awareness raising with potential users.

Guidance on Direct Payments

Two new guides aimed at increasing the number of people with learning disabilities using Direct Payments were published by the Department of Health in April 2004. In partnership with the Values into Action organisation, the Department of Health produced guidance for local authorities on how to make Direct Payments more accessible for people with learning disabilities. Values in Action Deputy Director Linsay McCulloch (cited in Unity Sale and Leason, 2004, p30) reported that the

> *Direct Choices: What councils need to do to make Direct Payments happen for people with learning disabilities'* (guidance was intended to) *bridge potential misunderstandings by local authorities and professionals about people with learning disabilities and Direct Payments.*

One of the most significant 'misunderstandings' about the eligibility of people with learning disabilities to Direct Payments is the issue of consent and the responsibility of management of the payments. The requirement that Direct Payments can only be made with the consent of the person involved was included in the original legislation to ensure that no-one would be forced to accept a Direct Payment that they did not want. The requirement to give consent was never intended to act as a barrier to Direct Payments, but rather as a safeguard for those people who preferred to receive services directly.

Instead, the 2003 guidance clarifies the issue is one of 'agreement' in that the person has to agree to the payment. Under the current legislation, as well as the draft Mental Capacity Bill, the following principles should apply.

- A person must be assumed to have capacity until established otherwise;

- 'All practicable steps' must be taken to help someone make a decision before deciding that they can't.

- Making an unwise decision is not to be taken as evidence that someone lacks capacity.

- All acts and decisions made for a person who lacks capacity must be in their best interests and should be the least restrictive alternative for that person's rights and freedoms.

(Winchester, 2004, p29)

Therefore, it cannot be assumed that a person generally lacks capacity to make decisions; nor can it be assumed that a person will be unable to have a Direct Payment on the basis that they may previously have been thought unable to make other decisions in their lives. Certainly, no groups of people should be excluded from receiving Direct Payments on blanket assumptions. Any authority that operates such policies leaves itself open to challenge, possibly resulting in judicial review (Ryan, 1999, cited in Joseph Rowntree Foundation findings, 1999, p2).

The *Direct Choices* guidance is clear that the purpose of Direct Payments is to increase people's independence and choice about how their needs are met. If a person can indicate a preference and can therefore express choice, and if these choices can be met through a Direct Payment, then this may well be the most appropriate option for that person. The guidance states that:

> *supporting people in making choices about how they want their needs to be met should be an integral part of the assessment and review process.*

> (DOH, 2004, p3)

Therefore, the decision to have a Direct Payment should be seen as a process rather than as a test that a person has to pass. A number of measures should be used in order to maximise the opportunity for a person to express choice and consent. These include:

- the provision of accessible information;
- giving people enough time to decide;
- using person centred approaches throughout the assessment and care planning process;
- considering the person's own views, wishes, aspirations and previous experiences;
- reducing the formalities by working with people in a familiar and relaxed environment of their choice;
- involving the person's support network or circle of support;
- using appropriate and imaginative methods to assist the person to indicate their preferences and choices (pictures, photographs, language, symbols, video and IT materials);
- use of advocates;
- not assuming initial uncertainty is an automatic refusal;
- taking an individual approach to consent, choice and the suitability of Direct Payments.

Once a person's agreement to a Direct Payment has been established, the guidance states that

> *the question of its management then needs to be addressed and councils have the responsibility to work with their partners to ensure that the right support is available.*

> (ibid., p4)

Undertaking Direct Payments involves many tasks and responsibilities such as the recruitment, employment and management of personal assistants; calculating wages and PAYE deductions; and preparing accounts for financial monitoring and audit. The provision of support is fundamental and the guidance is explicit in asserting that the person should have as much support as is required in order to manage Direct Payments, through the

> *duty to make Direct Payments to anyone who appears to be able to manage them (either alone or with support).*

(DOH, 2003, para. 47)

There are many ways in which a person with learning disabilities can be supported to manage their Direct Payments, the important factor is that it is tailored to the specific needs of the individual (Hasler, 2003, p11).

Glendinning et al. (2000, p209) report that most independent Direct Payment support services provide a range of support systems for users, including the provision of information and guidance; advocacy and advice; peer support and opportunities to share ideas and good practice with other users; training for users and personal assistants; payroll services; practical assistance in the recruitment and screening of potential workers. A key aspect of this is the importance that support services are commissioned with an emphasis on flexibility and the provision of support at whatever level is required. This will of course vary greatly, from the provision of long arm, occasional advice to regular and intensive practical support and assistance. Above all, the need for support should not be perceived as being problematic.

'Circles of support' can also be used to assist people with learning disabilities to express choices about their future and assist them to make decisions that affect their lives. A circle of support is a group of people who meet together on a regular basis to support a person to accomplish their goals in life. Antrobus (2001, p3) argues that

> *circles of support can be particularly productive for people with complex or greater support needs...to pursue a Direct Payment.*

The members of the circle, which may include family, friends or other community members, such as advocates, are involved because they admire and care enough about the 'focus' person to give their time and energy to helping the person overcome obstacles they may encounter and to increase the options available to them.

When it is assessed that a person does not have the capacity to consent to Direct Payments, the establishment of Independent Living Trusts can be used to give people more control over the ways their assistance is provided. Independent Living Trusts provide a structure which sets out the process for receiving payments from the local authority and arranging for services to assist the person. Trusts should provide legal safeguards and formalise arrangements for people with learning disabilities in order to facilitate supported decision-making and independent living arrangements, thus maximising the person's own control.

The *Direct Choices* guidance argues that *no-one can make good decisions on inadequate and incomplete information* (DoH, 2004, p7) and certainly, no-one is able to make a choice if they are not even aware of the scheme. The provision of accessible, relevant and easy to understand information is crucial to support people with learning disabilities to understand the options available to them and to enable them to make informed decisions and express an informed choice. As a response to this, in partnership with Values into Action, the DoH produced the Easy Guide to Direct Payments booklet, CD-Rom and cassette in

67

April 2004. In addition, the Direct Choices' guidance encourages local authorities to review their information and consult with users about their information needs as part of their Direct Payments promotion strategy.

The assessment process is fundamental in supporting people to make choices and take control over their own lives. Person centred planning is a key component of this and should inform the assessment process in the following ways:

- truly needs led assessment and care planning;

- risk assessment and risk management as a proactive response to risk taking;

- partnership working with the individual at the heart of the process…and full use of their networks and the people closest to them;

- person's own short and long term goals.

(ibid, p9)

The central principle should be that people with learning disabilities have a right to participate fully in their own assessment and that *what people want to do in their daily lives leads the agenda* (Clarke and Spafford, 2002, p255).

Conclusion

Direct Payments were lobbied for and introduced to facilitate greater choice, flexibility and independent living, and the reality is that through the use of Direct Payments, people with learning disabilities can be empowered to maximise their control over their own lives and their opportunities. In a recent study completed by the charity Scope (McMullen, 2003, p55), the majority of Direct Payment recipients cited choice and control as the key impact of Direct Payments on their lives:

I've got control, 100 per cent more control.

It gave me a home of my own.

It's given me freedom … make the decisions about my life.

However, there are individual, procedural, attitudinal, political and social forces that limit the extent to which they truly maximise choice and control. Whilst Direct Payments can provide choice and control in how people decide to meet their social care needs, they may be extremely limited in their housing options or how their health needs are met. People with learning disabilities have also experienced problems with opening bank accounts, a fundamental requirement for Direct Payments. Without such structures adopting flexible and person centred responses to people with learning disabilities, the true scope for choice and control remains extremely limited. Additionally, there is a need for a change in culture, values and attitudes if Direct Payments in particular, and independent living and user choice and control more generally, are to become a reality for people with learning disability. Essentially, as Spandler (2004, p205) argues,

the extent of their effectiveness may ultimately depend not only on local implementation but also on these wider forces.

Chapter 7
Caring for older people: informal care and carers

Keith Brown

INTRODUCTION

...providing the services and support which people who are affected by problems of ageing, mental illness, mental handicap or physical or sensory disability need to be able to live as independently as possible in their own homes or in 'homely' settings in the community.

(DoH, 1987)

The reshaping of community care envisaged by the architects of the 1990 NHS and Community Care Act is predicated on a continuation – indeed an expansion – of what is increasingly referred to as the 'informal welfare sector', (a term apparently popularised by the Wolfenden and Barclay Reports, 1978, 1982). Both the Griffiths Report, *Community Care: Agenda for Action* and the 1989 White Paper, *Caring for People*, stress its centrality and the need for local authorities to:

arrange the delivery of packages of care building first on the available contribution of informal carers and neighbourhood support.

(DHSS, 1989)

The significance attached to the domestic and communal production of welfare in the current 'restructuring' of health and welfare services has long been apparent. Indeed the blueprint for current proposals can be found in Norman Fowler's influential address to the Joint Social Services Conference in September 1984. Central to his concept of a *strategic and enabling role for social services departments* was the assertion that state provision of care should increasingly give way and tap into *a great reservoir of voluntary and private effort*. In the process he envisaged tens of thousands would be able to *give back something to their own community by participating in social support* (DHSS, 1984).

Fowler's promised Green Paper did not materialise, but the enhanced role of informal care remained a recurrent theme in policy statements and documents. As McCarthy argues, despite the protracted negotiations over agreeing the 'lead authority', a succession of reports throughout the 1980s have been

setting in train new processes of socialisation that would alter expectations and perceptions about the levels and nature of care.

(McCarthy, 1989, pp43–5)

Thus, to cite just a few examples – the 1981 Report, *Growing Older*; 1986 Cumberledge Report, *Neighbourhood Nursing*; 1987 White Paper, *Promoting Better Health* and parts of the Project 2000 scheme, all prompted both the notion of the 'enabling' state and the 'frontline' role of informal 'helping networks'. A similar process of acclimatising both users and providers to a more pluralist economy of welfare can be traced in a stream of national and local initiatives – some of which pre-date the Fowler speech (e.g. 1976 Good Neighbour Scheme, 1981 Care in the Community, 1984 Helping the Community Care).

The significance attached to informal welfare is not confined to Britain. Similar attempts to utilise and encourage the 'community' to support dependent individuals were a central feature of social policy in many European countries in the 1980s.

In France for instance, the 1988 Braun Report (*Les Personnes Agées Dependantes*) prioritised domiciliary support services for the elderly, and prompted both a more decentralised administrative system and greater coordination of statutory and independent health and welfare system providers and improved liaison with carers. (As in Belgium, families in France are legally responsible for the maintenance of their elderly relatives, and tax allowances reinforce this principle.) Deinstitutionalisation and an emphasis on 'home' care for other 'dependent' groups is a central feature of current social policy planning debates in other EEC states too, notably Italy, Belgium and Germany. In the US, recent attempts to residualise state welfare incorporated a wide-ranging campaign to highlight the crucial role of informal state welfare and self-provisioning. (Gilbert, 1983: David, in Levitas, 1986; Mangen, 1985; Hill, 1991; Baldock et al., 1990: Munday, 1989; Jamieson and Illsley, 1990).

In Sweden recent policy reviews have entailed paid leave for carers and the payment of carers. In Britain at a political level, and, indeed, in many of the responses to the 1990 Act, the value and potential of the informal sector remain unquestioned. Some commentators, however, have expressed considerable doubts about the assumed caring capacity of the 'community'. Whether such concerns are justified depends partly on one's assessment of research findings on the 'demand' for care, the current patterning of informal care and its growth potential. It also depends on one's concept of 'community care'. This paper aims to facilitate discussion of these key issues through a review both of empirical research and sociological discourse on 'community' in contemporary Britain. (Time constraints prevent a similar exploration of recent American and European studies.) It is hoped the concerns raised will facilitate consideration of the principles and practice of 'case management' and 'care packaging'.

Perspectives on 'community care' and 'informal care'

A cursory scan of the literature reveals considerable confusion and ambiguity in both nomenclature and use of the concept of 'informal care'. Indeed it is frequently used interchangeably with 'community care'. As numerous commentators have observed this, in turn, is a concept with infinitely *flexible meanings*. (Pascal, 1986, p86). Writing in the 1960s Titmuss highlighted both the normative and prescriptive elements of such an emotive term, seeing community care as characteristic of attempts *to employ idealistic terms to describe certain branches of public policy* entailing the danger that *in the public mind the aspirations of reformers are transmuted by touch of phrase into hardened reality* (Titmuss, 1968, p104).

Indeed reviewing the manifold definitional problems involved and the extent to which 'prescription' merges with 'description' one is tempted to agree with those who argue that the term *means little in itself* and should be abandoned – particularly in view of the *trail of confusion* created (Smith, 1989, p4).

Within sociology too the concept of community is often presented as *one of the most elusive and vague...now largely without specific meaning* (Abercrombie, 2006). Nevertheless it is possible to discern three major usages:

- it is used to refer to a locality/given geographical area;
- it is used to describe a local social system/set of social relationships which centre on a particular locality;
- it is employed to denote a type of relationship which is characterised by a strong sense of shared identity (based on common experiences/interests but not necessarily common residence).

The relevance of the first two usages to advance urban industrial societies has long been debated by sociologists, and a number have suggested that it is the third usage which most conforms to individual experiences in contemporary society, whilst the first are characteristic only of certain neighbourhoods and certain stages in the life cycle.

The concept of community care

Attempts to clarify the concepts of community and community care in policy terms have tended to concur in a distinction between two usages:

- care in the community (usually presented as the antithesis of institutional care);
- care by the community.

There is a general consensus that the policy of community care originated in the post-war reaction to institutional forms of care. This was evidenced in the 1940s in child care and from the 1950s in the treatment of the mentally ill, the elderly and the disabled. The twin pressures of cost efficiency and concern over the damaging effects of 'total institutions' (along with, in the case of the mentally ill, new drug treatments) led to a succession of measures designed to reduce institutional provision. With the 1959 Mental Health Act and more especially the 1962 Hospital Health Plan and the associated Health and Welfare Report of 1963, the contraction of traditional institutional care was 'connected' with residential units and non-residential services provided by local authorities (Quareshi and Walker, 1982 in op.cit, 1989; Jones, 1989, provide helpful surveys of these developments; a revisionist account, stressing pressures in the 1950's Ministry of Health to avoid the heavy costs of expanding and refurbishing inherited institutions, is provided by Goodwin, 1989/1990; 'feminist' accounts by Finch, in Ungerson, 1990; and Langan, 1990, develop a three phase chronological account).

As a plethora of studies have shown however, the first version of community care *existed largely at the level of political rhetoric*. It was:

> *never clearly and consistently defined, and the political will in the form of policy-making and planning machinery, and especially resource allocation and re-allocation were never mobilised.*

(Walker, in McCarthy, 1989, p205)

Despite repeated exhortations to local and health authorities to develop community based substitutes for institutional care, and the introduction of joint planning and funding in the late 1970s (belatedly including the voluntary sector), by the mid-1980s it was clear that *community care was grounded; more precisely it had never taken off* (Barritt, 1990, p9).

The manifest failure of the policy can be variously accounted for, with professional rivalry figuring high alongside political mismanagement in many accounts. (Indeed 'professional networks' may prove as crucial to case management in practice as the mobilisation of informal carers!). One factor which attracted increasing attention in the late 1970s, however, was the concept of community care implicit in the early measures. From the 1950s it appears that community care was perceived in terms of care provided by statutory agencies and their professional and ancillary personnel, primarily on a domiciliary basis, but also through 'homely' residential units, located in the 'community'. The latter continued to dominate both health and social service budgets and was included in DHSS programming from the 1970s. Nevertheless, the concept of care in the community conceived as non/less institutionalised provision, collectively funded and delivered by public agencies dominated official pronouncements.

The redefinition of community care

With the changed economic and ideological climate from the late 1970s, it appears that community care has been reconceptualised as care by the community:

> *Whatever level of public expenditure proves practicable, and however it is distributed, the primary sources of support and care are informal and voluntary ... It is the role of public authorities to sustain and where necessary to develop – but never to displace – such support and care. Care IN the community must increasingly mean care BY the community.*

(DHSS, 1981, p3)

A reading of the official documents and pronouncements suggests this is viewed as the provision of welfare and health care by relatives, neighbours, friends and other personal contacts. In one of the few early studies of such 'welfaring' Abrams provided what is probably still the most used definition:

> *'provision of help, support and protection by lay members of societies acting in everyday domestic and occupational settings.*

(Abrams, *Community Care, Policy and Politics*, 6, 1977, p25)

In this sense community care becomes transposed into informal care and it is this transposed version that appears to be uppermost in current policy-making (supplemented by voluntary and private market provision, either individually organised or 'packaged' by revamped local authorities).

This redefinition of community care can be seen simply as an acknowledgement of the failure of the earlier concept and a recognition of the extent to which the 'care gap' created by hospital closures and the under-development of local authority services for both those 'decanted' and 'non admissions' had apparently been filled by alternative care. As with the earlier 'anti institutionalism' it can also be read as an attempt to ensure more 'natural' support for dependent groups. It is also possible, however, to interpret this redefinition of community care as intrinsic to *a new era of welfare that owes as much to the mores and values of the market as it does to social service and care* (McCarthy,1989, p9).

Patterns of caring: family based care

However one perceives the 'mixed economy of welfare' envisaged by the 1990 Act, its implementation is conditional on the continued – and expanding – support of the informal sector. Yet despite an upsurge in research in the last decade, an understanding of the characteristics and functioning of the helping networks available to dependent individuals in non-residential care is still uneven.

Ideally, any assessment should encompass not only types of relationship (family/other etc), the number, range, frequency and duration of contacts between the 'cared for' and 'carer(s)', the tasks undertaken and services provided, but also the meanings attached to the relationship by the different participants. By its very nature however, much of the help provided is currently unrecorded and also extremely difficult to both access and quantify let alone assess. Nevertheless the redirection of policy is now spawning a mass of research, both 'micro' and 'macro'. In particular, detailed analyses of the 1985 General Household Survey and the OPCSS Disablement Survey are appearing, giving new insight into both the numbers and characteristics of various 'dependent' groups and those who identified themselves as 'carers' (i.e. individuals who *look after or give special help to or provide some regular service or help for any sick, handicapped person, adult or child*). Many of the key findings have been usefully collated by Parker (1985, 1990). Further summaries are provided by Evandrou, 1990; Twigg, 1989; and Perring, 1989.

Evandrou's GHS survey leads her to estimate that 14 per cent of those over 16, i.e. one in seven adults or six million people, were caring for a sick, handicapped or older person. Parker endorses the six million figure for Great Britain, but argues that only 3.7 million should be seen as 'helping' adults disabled enough to be included in the OPCS survey, with 1.3 million as 'main carers' (as in her 1985 estimate). Indeed, there is now considerable debate over both the numbers and characteristics of 'carers' (Redding, 1991).

Most research has focused on 'family' care rather than that of friends or neighbours. Before reviewing the main findings however, it is crucial to recognise that the term 'family', like 'community', is open to different interpretations. Conventionally, sociologists have long distinguished between the nuclear and extended family. Traditionally, the former was perceived in terms of a married couple plus their offspring, the unspoken assumption being that the couple comprised a male breadwinner and a female 'homemaker'.

It is contestable whether this family form was ever the norm, and current research clearly demonstrates that the 'cereal packet' image is now only one of a diversity of family structures in contemporary society. It appears however, that much social legislation is still permeated by 'traditionalist' concepts of both the nuclear family and its links with extended kin – and such thinking seems to underpin the care by the community programme. The compatibility between this and current/projected family trends will be raised later. For now, recognition of this pluralism is the essential backcloth to any research review. Indeed some sociologists prefer to refer to household rather than family to explicate the patterning of care.

Themes in family care

Drawing on the newly available studies it is possible to distinguish a number of common themes in family care. First, a substantial body of research, stretching back to the 1950s, has attempted to demythologise the frequently repeated assertion that state welfare has undermined family care for dependants. Hadley and Hatch encapsulated the general finding:

> *Most of the care that is provided for dependent people living in their own homes comes not from the state, nor from voluntary organisations, nor from commercial sources, but from family, friends and neighbours.*

(Hadley and Hatch, 1981, p87)

This general conclusion has been endorsed by a stream of family studies in the 1980s. Often a by-product of (feminist inspired) concern at the differential employment patterns of men and women, such studies have documented the care provided in or through the family for a range of client groups. Moreover, recent historical research suggests that the contemporary family is providing more support than in the past (Wall, *Families and the Community*, Soc Sci News, 7, 1990).

Secondly, studies of different dependent groups, while emphasising differential needs, have also identified a number of common strands in the patterning of family resourced care.

Household/non household based care
Evandrou's data suggests 1.7 million adults care for a 'co-resident'; 4.25 million for someone outside their household (four per cent all adults/10%).

Highly dependent on one primary carer
Though this was implicit in earlier research and emphasised by studies of 'single' carers, its prevalence within families is only now being documented. It appears that once an individual is perceived as the carer, support from other relatives (and friends) tends to disappear. The processes whereby such *invisible* carers *emerge* has been explored by Ungerson (1987) who stresses the role of co/proximate residence, age, other commitments and especially gender in this process. Evandrou (1990) suggests females are more likely to be *sole* carers; males peripheral carers, though *joint* caring is less *skewed*. The first are most likely to be caring for spouses; peripheral carers for other relatives/friends, and joint carers for a parent-in-law. Sole carers are likely to be the most *disadvantaged* in natural terms and also the most *stressed*.

The gendered nature of care

Initial research into various client groups in the 1980s suggested that *the majority of carers are women* and *the majority of women will at some time in their lives be carers* (Equal Opportunites Commission, 1982, piii). This division of labour appeared to operate along several dimensions:

- in terms of the numbers of female/male carers;

- in terms of the age at which caring starts/length of the caring 'career';

- in terms of the source of the relationship (males tend to care for spouses; females for other relatives too);

- in terms of the type of tasks and services provided;

- in terms of the amount and length of time spent caring;

- in terms of support from other family members/ contacts;

- in terms of help from statutory/other sources.

The general conclusion of the early studies is well summarised in the notion of 'the double equation':

> *in practice, community care equals care by family, and in practice care by the family equals care by women.*

(Finch and Groves, 1980, p494)

It appeared to run counter to equal opportunities legislation!

A number of studies explored the differential pressures underpinning this division of labour and related taboos surrounding 'cross-sex caring'. While some have focused on the complexities of family history and inter-personal relationships in determining 'caring', most are framed in terms of different feminist analyses (Dalley, 1988; Lewis and Meredith, 1988).

Male carers

In contrast some recent studies, notably those of Arber and Gilbert (1989) suggest men make a larger contribution than has been recognised and – in the case of the infirm elderly – it is household type (single/couple/presence of unmarried younger members) rather than gender which determines external support. Evandrou too argues that *men are far more involved in providing informal care than previously thought* (1990, p.29). Indeed, 2.5 million of the 6 million carers in her study were male. Parker's research review however, leads her to conclude that, *in the population at large, women provide the bulk of care* and that there has been *little shift in the division of care* (1990, p56). The relative role of the 'new male' in this – as other areas of family life is likely to remain controversial. What is clear, however, is that the majority of male carers are caring for spouses – care of others is still primarily, in practice, a female task. It may also be that the form of survey/questioning used in some studies leads to higher male self reporting, with women taking care work more for granted.

The costs of care

As has been frequently noted the impulse to both versions of 'community care' has been primarily cost driven. From the outset 'care in the community' was seen as a cheaper as well as a more therapeutic and personalised alternative to institutionalisation.

It is also clear from official sources that 'care by the community' is seen as ensuring 'affordable' cost effective care. But again, most studies testify an implicit 'creative accountancy' which fails to quantify the hidden costs of informal care. For the prime carer, these 'costs' are now well established if unmitigated.

- The cost in terms of the drain on carers' physical health.
- The impact on carers' mental health.
- The stress placed on marital and other family relationships.
- The loss of employment opportunities, both short and long term, and the associated reduction in current and life time earnings.
- The extra financial costs entailed in servicing the varied special needs of 'cared for' individuals.
- The loss of social contacts and 'non-obligated time'.

Evandrou suggests carers as a group are likely to experience relative impoverishment, but that sole carers have a *higher probability* of low income, with female sole carers being *particularly disadvantaged*. Carers with co-resident dependants were more likely to experience poverty than those caring for someone outside the home (1990, p1). As feminists such as Land and Graham have frequently argued, caring, particularly when undertaken by women, sustains not one but two forms of dependency. Ironically, as Glendinning's recent research shows, the carer can become financially dependent on the cared for – and face further impoverishment on the latter's decease or admission to permanent care, (see e.g. Land, in Bulmer, 1989; Glendinning and Baldwin, 1988; Glendinning, 1990).

The quality of family care

Most research has tended to focus on the carer's perspectives, though this 'imbalance' is now beginning to be rectified, notably by Quareshi and Walker's *The Caring Relationship* (1989). What emerges from this – as other studies, is the highly variable nature of both the rewards and the strains inherent in caring. By its very nature, any assessment of the quality of such care, grounded as it is in pre-existing relationships and separate from the performance indicators currently being developed for formal services is obviously highly subjective. One salient conclusion, neglected in much of the debate about community care, but familiar to those involved in child care, is that family care can be both *the best and the worst form of care* (ibid, p240). (It is perhaps worth noting that two 'elder abuse' journals are already being published in the USA.) It is also worth noting that several recent studies suggest many of the cared for prefer some degree of reciprocity in relation to their carers. Indeed the few user based investigations suggest many of those diagnosed as mentally ill have more positive perceptions of institutional care than that provided in/by *the community* (Chapman et al.,1991).

Caring for Different Forms of Dependency

Within these overall general patterns, however, it is crucial to recognise that expectations and practices about who should care, and where, vary with the type and age of the dependant. Disabled children are seen as primarily a parental (in practice maternal) responsibility. However, attitudes towards the care of adults diverge according to whether the disability/illness develops after a 'normal' life in old age, or whether it was manifest in childhood. While the role of the prime carer within the family is now well recognised in each area, what is not clear is the possible variability of other relatives' support according to the nature of the dependency.

'Neighbouring' and 'helping networks'

In contrast to the morass of research into family centred care, the notion of a surrounding layer of informal carers has, with a few notable exceptions, remained until very recently, largely untested. The indirect evidence supplied by the numerous family studies, however, suggests that the contribution of non-relatives is generally minimal and highly restricted both in terms of the quantity and quality of support offered. General studies of friendship patterns and local social structures (not necessarily emanating from concern with social policy) provide insights into the constraints on this wider source of informal care.

For instance Allan, like many others, emphasises two distinctive characteristics of friendship: friends (unlike kin and neighbours) are chosen, and the relationship hinges on reciprocity. One's friends must bring *equivalent financial and emotional resources to the relationship* and while 'caring about' may be a facet of the relationship 'caring for' is not an inherent component (Allan, 1985, p137). In his more recent, extended attempt to initiate a sociology of friendship, (including class/gender/ethnic/life cycle differences) he reiterates the *short termism* of many friendships, the many circumstantial constraints which prevent friends caring for either a dependent individual or a carer, and above all the intrinsically reciprocal exchange base of contemporary friendship patterns, the symmetry of which is disrupted by *a continuing need for unilateral care* (Allan, 1990, p113).

Neighbours may become friends, but this is usually based on some form of reciprocity too, involving (alongside 'socialising') restricted exchanges of such services as looking after the property or keys during one's absence, offering lifts or babysitting and borrowing and lending of various kinds. The extent of such neighbouring emerges from a wealth of community studies. As one of the most indefatigable investigators into local networks, Wilmott suggests such 'support' is not easily translated into 'caring'. This emerges clearly from his useful classification of different forms of informal care:

- personal care/tending /human maintenance;
- domestic care;
- auxiliary care;
- social support;
- surveillance.

Given the reciprocity inherent in neighbouring it appears that the restricted and short term categories (social support) and (surveillance) involving low emotional investment and personal commitment are those most likely to be resourced by neighbours. Even here however, such help is patchy (Wilmott, 1986; Sharkey, 1989; Wenger, 1990).

Quareshi and Walker's Sheffield study leads to the same conclusion as does Finch's, (1989). Such findings were anticipated by Abrams' pioneering studies. These led him to reject *romanticised notions* of spontaneous altruism in favour of the notion that care-giving *is a self interested activity*. Non-kin (and even family care) in contemporary society was *typically volatile, spasmodic and unreliable* and *invariably tied to perceptions of long or short term reciprocal advantage* (Abrams, 1977, pp125–132). The recent edition of his – and others' – research into 'good neighbourhood' schemes support his earlier findings, highlighting the emergence of 'new neighbourhoodism' consequent on post-war housing developments. Most people, he argued, live in new neighbourhoods and their relationships are not only highly privatised but instrumental – participation in locally based mutual aid being contingent on a calculation of likely costs/benefits. The only features of traditional neighbourliness to have survived, he concluded, were *mothers and gossip*! In such circumstances, attempts to revive/draw on local social networks appeared *misguided* (Bulmer, 1986; 1987). It could be argued that even in the 'classic slum' setting or small hamlet where shared residence and experiences appear to have fostered neighbourly interdependence, recent research provides *little evidence to support the idea that non-kin played a major part in caring, except in times of crisis* (Allan, 1990). More significant now however, is the common concern in many studies that contemporary lifestyles and residential patterns disable even limited neighbouring.

The role of personal social services/SSDs

From the Barclay Report on, there has been pressure to interweave informal and statutory care, but most research documents a mismatch between the latter and the essentially female based pattern of informal care (contributing to attempts at improved planning and delivery). Writing in 1985, Parker concluded that

> *available services are likely to have little overall effect for informal carers. Firstly, few dependent people who have carers appear to receive services, and when they do such services are crisis-oriented rather than part of long-term support. Secondly, the criteria by which services are allocated are often irrational (not allocated in relation to need) and discriminatory (not provided where female carers are available).*

> (Parker, 1985, p88)

Both the Short Report and the Audit Commission (1986) reached similar conclusions, and the former also drew attention to the neglect of the particular needs of ethnic minority carers and their dependants. Reviewing conventional health and welfare provision in 1990, Parker still found they *have little overall effect for informal carers*, repeating the same points made in 1986 (1990, p125). Her findings have been endorsed by Twigg et al., (1990). Despite initiatives such as carers' forums, carers' handbooks, family hospitality and other 'sit-in' schemes *genuine support for carers is far from the norm* (1990, p60).

Under-resourcing and inter-professional rivalry is held partly responsible for this mismatch. But a number of studies suggest it is also a reflection of *received ideas* among health and social workers about both 'dependency' and informal caring, the latter being conceived primarily as a female responsibility (Rojek, 1988; Quareshi and Walker 1989; Dalley, 1988). A further factor appears to be the prevalence of received ideas on the family patterns of different ethnic groups in Britain (Atkin, 1991).

Twigg has developed a provisional classification of the frames of reference used by health and especially social workers in dealing with carers. As she emphasises, care is usually structured around the client with concern for the carer being a more 'instrumental' by-product of this. In her ideal type construction, a care workers' model of the carer can take three possible forms:

- carers as resources (though undirectable and uncommandable);

- carers as co-workers;

- carers as co-clients.

All three, however, entail a common tension generated by a concept of success which takes *passage into residential care as a crucial service indicator* and thus, from a carer's perspective can appear to *reward failure* (Twigg, 1989, pp62–3, also in Jamieson and Illsley, 1990). Recent studies of the carer-service provider interface suggest a further dimension, that of the carer as co-claimant/advocate. Assumption of this role, however, is contingent on the carers' knowledge-base and the promotional/intervention strategies of SSDs. Carers' potential as a pressure group however, may well be restricted by factors similar to those inhibiting industrial action among low waged female workers! (Hunter and Macpherson, in Jamieson and Illsley, 1990).

Social protection and informal care

This has been a much neglected aspect of informal care. But a growing number of studies are now exploring the correspondence/lack of correspondence between the financial costs and dependency/caring and the support systems available. The potential for carers to become financially dependent on the cared for and the life-cycle/pension entitlements implications for women carers taking career breaks/part-time employment have already been raised (see too: e.g. Glendinning, 1990; Finnister, 1991). Many studies echo Johnson's finding that the current emphasis on community and family care *might be more acceptable if statutory financial support for families were more generous* and the needs of both carers/cared for were recognised rather than undermined by recent social security measures (Johnson, *The Mixed Economy of Welfare*, in Ware and Goodin, 1990, p148). Indeed it is frequently presented as not only more 'natural' and less rigid than bureaucratic/professional public care systems, but as preserving the independence of the individual concerned. It is perhaps worth considering whether family care necessarily reduces dependence.

The caring capacity of the community

Whatever the specifics of research into the parameters of informal care however, in Britain its significance appears unquestioned. The assumption central to current policy, that it provides an under-used and expandable reservoir of care capable of meeting the increase in dependency projected by both the 'ageing' of Britain and the increased incidence/survival of other dependants, is also questionable. Johnson captures this new concern, suggesting that

> we should be asking not whether the family can provide more care in the future but whether it will even be able to maintain its current level of provision.

(Johnson, 1990, p127)

Moreover:

> The wholesale transfer of responsibility from the state to informal carers, which some New Right theorists advocate, is likely to lead to falling standards of care and intolerable pressures on families. There are limits to the extra work which families can absorb, and those limits may already have been reached. The informal sector is in no position to compensate for a reduction in the state's role. Indeed, if informal care is to continue at its present level, state support of the family will have to be increased.

(Johnson, in Ware and Goodin, 1990, p151)

Such concerns are not confined to Britain – a recent European study of family patterns concluded

> the traditional sources of family care for all vulnerable members can no longer be taken for granted, implying a growing bill for ...governments.

(Robbins, 1990, p103)

Feminist writers in particular have highlighted the extent to which shifts in population age structures, employment patterns and family relationships (including rising divorce rates) indicate possible problems in sustaining informal care work in the future. Other research into kinship networks raises similar concerns about the changing pattern of such relationships. Wilmott, for instance, suggests there are *three broad kinship arrangements* in contemporary Britain: *the local extended family* (characteristic of one in eight of the adult population), *the dispersed extended family* (characteristic of half the adult population) and *the attenuated extended family*, (Wilmott, 1987).

Reviewing studies of the 'informal sector', Allan concludes

> any attempt to influence networks of neighbours, friends, and kin so as to encourage greater support and caring for members in need would not be so much an extension of 'natural' networks as a wholly artificial manipulation of them.

(Davies, 1991, p121)

Moreover, as Foster argues, *there is very little reason to suppose that non-compulsory altruism will break out* amongst 'non-carers', (Foster, *Residential Care of Frail Elderly People: a Positive Re-assessment*, SP and A, 25, 2, 1991).

In response to such concerns, and as part of the wider effort to create non-sexist welfare policies and practices, some are advocating greater use of residential and/or paid domiciliary care. This however, is conceived in 'non-traditional', gender-neutral terms and also emphasises customised consumerist practices. (Finch, 1984; Dalley, 1988; Foster, 1991).

The feasibility and modes of improving the position of carers, whilst both *weakening sexual divisions in caring*, and *maximising opportunities for independence for older people or those with disabilities* is currently highly controversial, and a range of possible measures are being canvassed, including new financial schemes for both carers and cared for, (see • e.g. Baldwin and Twigg, in Mclean and Groves, 1991; Glennesterm et al., 1990, and, from a different perspective, Ramon, 1991, which emphasises the need to incorporate a multi-dimensional concept of 'normalisation', into both policy and practice in the 'new' community care regime.) Most, however, assume a state rather than a market-based commercially driven response, emphasising the need for more innovative delivery systems not the abandonment of public provision *in favour of some idealised and unrealistic notion of family care* (Jamieson and Illsley, 1991, p19).

One's response depends on how one interprets current demographic and social trends, and on one's assessment of some of the alternative concepts and models of care that are currently being canvassed. However, it is clear that in the twenty-first century the pressure on the state to provide care for vulnerable adults is rapidly growing as the capacity of the informal carers is under greater pressure. Changes in family structure, the need for potential informal carers to work full time to pay for mortgages and associated housing costs, and also to ensure they have sufficient pension provision for the future, coupled with a society which appears to be moving more towards a moral position that reduces the perception of a moral duty/responsibility to care for one's relatives, all put further pressure on the state as the potential pool of informal carers contracts.

Addendum

Since this chapter was originally written, there have been a number of changes that impact on informal care. The issues raised in this chapter are still relevant to current social work policy, however, and in order to help the reader the following should be noted.

The economic contribution of carers has recently been estimated at £57 billion and continues to be increasingly recognised by government. Informal carers are now seen as vital providers in the mixed economy of care (Carvel, 2005). Indeed, as Carvel (2005) points out, there are more carers than people working in the NHS and Social Services combined.

Following the Conservative government's Carer's (Recognition and Services) Act 1995, giving carers the right to assessment of their own needs, New Labour continued with The Carers National Strategy, Caring for Carer's (DoH, 1999). The stated aim is to support carers to continue caring, to protect their health and well-being, and giving carers rights to assess services in their own rights. Following this, the Carer and Disabled Children Act (CDCA) 2000 gave powers to local authorites to provide services to carers including Direct Payments, following an assessment. The recent Green paper Independence, Well-being and Choice 2005 further strengthens this role with its focus on carers' rights to social inclusion, employment, leisure and well-being.

Of note though is that according to Lyon (2005) the CDCA (2000) gave local authorities 'power' rather than a 'statutory duty' to provide carers Direct Payments (DP). Only 25 per cent of local authorities were found to be offering carers Direct Payments (ADSS Survey 2005 quoted by Lyon, 2005). Hudson (2005) further went on to report that there was a high level of dissatisfaction with carer assessment from the carers' perspective.

Thus we see a continuing picture of pressure and demand on informal carers despite recent changes in legislation and systems designed to offer greater support.

In summary, the following questions are asked.

- Will informal carers be able or willing to continue to provide the current level of care they now provide in the future?

- What are the implications of any changes to the level and volume of informal care on society, social work practice and the individuals being cared for?

Chapter 8

Promoting inclusiveness: developing empowering practice with minority groups of older people – the example of older lesbian women and gay men

Lee-Ann Fenge

INTRODUCTION

Recognising the diversity of experience within the British ageing population has been supported by recent policy which promotes person-centred and anti-ageist practice (*National Service Framework for Older People*, 2001). The theme of meeting the needs of a diverse population is also supported by the government's recent Green Paper on adult social care, Independence, Well-being and Choice (2005, page 9). However, older lesbians and gay men to date have received little interest from service providers and British research has only started to appear in recent years.

Background

Historically, social work departments have structured their work with older people on the basis of ageist assumptions, over-simplifying their needs as being routine, and using largely unqualified staff to assess the needs of older service users (Hugman, 1994). Although paying lip service to the older person's views, the assessment may not be focused around the individual's experience and expertise. Structuring interviews using increasingly complex assessment tools and forms compromises the user's perspective further (Dill, 1993).

Central to social work practice with older lesbian women and gay men is their liberation from dominant knowledge and power practices, and this requires the development of new knowledge from research to improve practitioners', understanding of the needs of this diverse group. This is particularly important for 'minority' groups of older people who have traditionally been invisible from mainstream service provision. Postmodernism has evolved a worldview that acknowledges there is no one way of knowing, no one way of being, and no one way of experiencing reality (Warburton, 1994). It is therefore important to open up social work's professional knowledge base to critical scrutiny (Pease, 2002), and to embrace knowledge that evolves from *inside a culture* (Swantz, 1996, p124), rather than being purely defined by 'outside' professional knowledge and language. This supports the development of research methods which engage with older lesbians and gay men to enable them to steer the research and growing evidence base in this area of practice.

The impact of ageism

Ageism represents a key feature of the discrimination and oppression that all older people experience, and therefore the fundamental basis of practice with older people must be anti-ageist. Central to this is recognising that older people as a group are subject to discrimination and oppression on both macro and micro levels within society (Thompson, 1998). The National Service Framework for Older People (2001) in Britain has highlighted the need to tackle ageist practice within health and social care, but to implement this policy challenges need to be made concerning the negativity associated with ageing at personal, cultural and structural levels within society.

A society that reflects negative images about ageing and older people will have a negative impact on those who are older and drives a wedge between the young and old. The image of frailty and vulnerability in old age is powerful (Herring and Thom, 1997), and influences how both the public and practitioners view older people. Practitioners can underestimate the impact of ageism on older people, and this can increase the dehumanisation that many older people experience (Milner and O'Byrne, 1998). As a result older people can be seen as non-persons, their needs and views being overlooked by professionals who see themselves as expert in defining their needs and developing service provision.

Another key feature of ageism is that it categorises older people as a homogenous group (Thompson and Thompson, 2001) and diversity of experience and difference is lost in stereotypical assumptions about ageing and decline. Therefore some older people may face further discrimination and oppression on the basis of their gender, sexuality, ethnicity or disability.

In Britain, Age Concern has raised the profile of the needs of older lesbian women and gay men through its publication *Opening Doors* (2001). This report suggests that one in every 15 users of Age Concern services in England is a lesbian woman or gay man. However, to date, there has been no UK research on sizeable samples of older gay men and lesbians, and the research that has emerged is on people living in the USA. Langley (1997) undertook a small scale study on behalf of Age Concern Brighton which highlighted the oppression experienced and feared at a personal, cultural and structural level (p1). It is therefore vitally important to challenge negative attitudes as well as looking to develop service provision for these groups in the future.

Sexuality

Oppression is a key feature in the lives of older lesbian women and gay men. Oppression is experienced not only through ageism but may also be experienced through heterosexism (Berkman and Zinberg, 1997) which permeates our culture and social institutions, and through homophobia (Hudson and Ricketts, 1980).

For the first time in history two distinct groups of older lesbians and gay men are co-existing in society. The first group are older lesbians and gay men, who as a result of growing up in an extremely homophobic period, during which homosexuality was viewed as criminal, sinful and sick (Cook-Daniels, 1997), are a hidden population. Many have lived with the fear that exposure would devastate their lives and many have felt isolated and ashamed of their feelings (Bohan, 1996). As homosexuality was illegal in Britain until 1963 and a mental disorder until 1973, many will have endured medical interventions (D'Augelli et al, 2001) or been prosecuted. This is likely to have resulted in feelings of stigma and shame, which has gone on to shape their lives (Brotman, et al. 2003). In order to live in safety many gay men acquired a wife and had discreet sexual relations with men. For women, society deemed living with female roommates as acceptable and thus they often passed as this and nothing more (Quam, 1993).

The effects of living a concealed life can however be seen as having a lasting detriment, as some individuals continue to feel abnormal. After concealing a large part of themselves for the majority of their lives, many are still coming to terms with the effects of homophobia, including low self-esteem, a fear of disclosing their sexuality and a loss of relationships with family and friends (Hays et al, 1997). This may prevent some people who think of themselves as gay and lesbian as identifying themselves as such due to the stigma associated with the labels (Martin and Knox, 2000). It may also prevent them from approaching social services and other agencies when in need (Jacobs et al, 1999).

The second group has arisen not because of an increase in the number of lesbians and gay men, but because, for the first time in history, a generation will retire who have lived most of their lives as *out* lesbians or gay men (Beeler et al, 1999). 'Coming out' can be seen as a process of developing awareness and acknowledgement of homosexual thoughts and feelings, and results in public awareness of one's identity (Davies, 1996).

One of the predominant factors determining how older lesbians and gay men adjust to ageing is how they feel about their sexuality. D'Augelli et al (2001) found that individuals with a positive view towards their sexuality had better mental health, which was echoed by Deacon et al (1995) who reported that high life satisfaction and low self-criticism related to feeling positive about being gay. Research has shown that older lesbians and gay men who cope less well with ageing are commonly those with an internalised homophobia, developed through keeping their sexuality a secret. Because of this secrecy, many individuals felt guilty and ashamed, which when internalised and not resolved, inevitably leads to low self-esteem, greater social isolation (Jacobs et al 1999) and poor mental health (D'Augelli et al 2001).

Developing awareness

For practitioners, it is important to be aware of the social construction of sexuality and the impact that religion, social and political beliefs and values have on the way older lesbian women and gay men are perceived by society. For example, managing stigma and exposure to discrimination over long periods of time has also been shown to result in higher risks of depression and suicide, addictions and substance abuse (Brotman et al, 2003). However, other research has suggested that 80 per cent of women and 62 per cent of men felt that their sexuality had enriched their lives (Heaphy et al, 2003). The experience of stigma is not just an individual experience, but can be seen as a tool of social inequality which reinforces the social exclusion of certain groups within society, and therefore power inequality is an important part of this experience (Parker and Aggleton, 2003).

The impact of 'heterosexism' is that service providers have traditionally tailored their services to meet the needs of the heterosexual population (Jacobs et al., 1999). Although older lesbian women and gay men have the same needs as heterosexual older people, they will have experienced ageing differently. Therefore they require health and social care services that respond to their own particular needs. This includes the importance of spending as much time with and being supported by fellow gay men and lesbian women (Langley,1997, Beeler et al, 1999).

Social work practitioners therefore need to develop their awareness of the invisibility and oppression experienced by older gay men and lesbian women, and also develop sensitivity to allow them to voice their experiences and share their situated knowledge in order to develop practice and service provision. Recognition of and valuing difference is central to this process.

Empowerment

Empowerment, although 'a contested concept' (Means and Smith, 1998, p70) has been seen to be *the keystone of social work* (Lee, 2000, p34).There are a number of radical perspectives on empowerment including those which talk of empowerment in terms of *challenging and combating oppression* (Ward and Mullender, 1991, p22) and those which equate it with being able to exercise power or take control of oneself (Braye and Preston-Shoot, 1995, p48). This perhaps can be broadly seen to link into notions of 'citizenship' and 'rights'. One way of viewing citizenship is in terms of participation, and as such participation *can be seen as representing an expression of human agency* (Lister, 1998, p27). This could be seen in terms of political activity or voting, but also through less formal means such as participation in local community activities, family life, or social work assessment processes.

The inability to 'participate', or restrictions placed on participation, is central to this discussion. For many older people participation may be prevented by ageist assumptions about the value of older people within society and the negative connotations attached to ageing within a western culture, and older gay men and lesbian women may be excluded further by discrimination and oppression related to gender or sexuality.

Researchers have identified the *invisibility* of older gay men and lesbians, both within and outside the gay and lesbian community (Wahler and Gabbay, 1999, Fullmer et al., 1999). Some suggest that like the older population in general, older gay and lesbians are often socially isolated, and that they find themselves *disengaged* from the lesbian and gay community (Jacobs et al., 1999). The stereotypical image of the ageing gay man includes someone who is *excluded* from a *youthist* gay culture, lonely, sexless and depressed (Kelly, 1977, Wahler and Gabbay, 1999). Similar negative stereotypes exist for older lesbians including being lonely, asexual and unattractive (Berger, 1982, Fullmer et al., 1999). Within the homosexual community, these negative stereotypes may set older people apart from the younger members of the community and add to their invisibility. The idealisation of youth which may be common within the gay community may drive a wedge between young and old and may displace older gay men from the social spaces previously open to them within the gay community (Murray and Adam, 2001). A focus on 'citizenship' can therefore help to promote emancipatory forms of social work practice which highlight rights to participation and inclusion.

Emancipatory approaches to social work practice focus on social change at both an individual and structural level. Anti-oppressive practice is central to this approach and offers a person-centred philosophy and egalitarian value system (Dominelli, 1993, p24). Anti-oppressive practice therefore requires 'power sharing', and a move away from approaches which focus on the expertise of the practitioner to those which focus on the participation and expertise of the service user. It is not the case that older individuals choose not to participate, as might be suggested by decline models of ageing and approaches such as disengagement theory (Cumming and Henry, 1961), but that they are prevented from doing so by a society that views youth as premium and old age as a time of invisibility and dependency *which takes away adult status and personhood of the elderly* (Featherstone and Wernick, 1995).

Social work practice

Recent changes in policy concerning older people have influenced the process of assessment and practice. The Single Assessment Process, which was introduced in the National Service Framework for Older People (2001), is aimed at ensuring a more person centred approach to assessment, whilst encouraging professionals to work much more closely together. This aims to replace the fragmented and repetitive assessments that older people have experienced at the hands of health and social care professionals, by one 'seamless' process. This approach values person-centred care and independence, and the older person's views and wishes should be central to the assessment process.

Good practice is suggested by adopting a user narrative approach in the form of a biography in the older person's own words. The idea of a *critical dialogue* (Freire, 1972) can be seen as important within this process as it centres upon the notion of sharing and acknowledgment. This can be seen as an important principle both within practice and research with older gay men and lesbian women as it values diversity of experience and meaning (Pollner and Rosenfeld, 2000).

This may enable older gay men and lesbian women to 'co-author' their assessments using language they choose to represent themselves. This may include whether or not to 'come out' to the assessor. This narrative approach is supported by research by Richards (2000), which supports the focus on user perspective. She suggests that it

> *will tend to reduce the power imbalance between elders and practitioners, as practitioners strive to engage with the elderly person's perspective instead of expecting them to fit into bureaucratic and professional agendas and ways of thinking.*

(p47)

Narratives allow service users to tell and retell stories about their lives, and this can be used to challenge and deconstruct dominant cultural stories that can serve to oppress them (Milner, 2001). However, much may depend on the skill of the practitioner involved in the assessment, and a consequence of greater interprofessional working may mean that the assessment is not led by a social worker, but by another professional involved in the care of the older person.

Some criticisms have been made suggesting that although 'biography' is central to the new assessment process, an over focus on 'medical' needs rather than personal and social needs will detract from the service users' participation in the process (Hunter, 2001). It does raise the issue of user participation, particularly if the workers undertaking these assessments at a contact level are untrained and rely heavily on format driven assessments. A further concern is raised by research that suggests that older lesbian women and gay men may be reluctant to approach health and social care providers because of a belief that organisations assume all their clients are heterosexual and have a lack of awareness about gay and lesbian issues, leading to inaccurate assessments and inappropriate provision (Jacobs et al, 1999). This is in part supported by research, which has reported instances of overt discrimination, disclosure, neglect and policy insensitivity (Bohan, 1996; Moore, 2000; Cook-Daniels, 1997).

The extension of the 1996 Community Care (Direct Payments Act) in 2000 to include people aged 65 and over to benefit from Direct Payments may offer older gay men and lesbian women the opportunity to make choices in the type of care they choose (Langley, 2001). However research by Killin (1993) points to additional issues for older gay men and lesbian women within the context of Direct Payments. These issues include homophobia by employed personal assistants, or the personal assistant not adhering to the principle of confidentiality and disclosing the sexual orientation of the cared for person.

Responsibilities

Both of the above developments raise the issue of training and guidance for local authority staff, health authority staff and unqualified personal assistant staff in the process of assessment and the implementation of Direct Payment schemes. Issues around diversity and choice require particular attention and increased consideration of the barriers faced by people who are gay or lesbian is essential to this process (Glasby and Littlechild, 2002).

Research suggests that practitioners should take an individual responsibility to become aware of how older lesbians and gay men function within both gay and non-gay cultures

(Jacobs et al, 1999). They need to become more informed about the realities of same-sex relationships and issues relating to being gay and growing old (Hays et al, 1997) and to become skilled at addressing clients' fears and needs. This could include having an awareness of legal realities and finding respectful providers.

The Civil Partnership Act 2004 is being implemented which will lessen the impact of inequality previously experienced by same sex partners and ensure employment and benefit rights. For many older lesbians and gay men, the lack of partnership rights has caused economic insecurity, a difficulty that may already be pertinent for older lesbians who are among the poorest group in Britain (single women 65+). This is partly due to traditional low paid part-time employment (Wilton, 1997), however even full time female workers have been disadvantaged due to unequal pay and pensions (Bayliss, 2000). Lesbians (and gay men) to date have been unlikely to benefit from a partner's pension and as women generally live longer, individual pensions are markedly lower than they are for men.

Conclusion

Recent policy has raised the profile of older people, promoting person-centred and anti-ageist practice. However the pervasive nature of ageism at not only the personal but cultural and structural levels (Thompson and Thompson, 2001) means that older people tend to be treated as a homogenous group. Diversity of experience is lost in stereotypical assumptions about the negative consequences of ageing, and there is a risk that those from minority groups remain hidden and forgotten.

The challenge for social work practice and research is to adopt approaches which encourage partnership with service users, to develop new knowledge and understanding for developing practice with minority groups in the twenty-first century.

This requires developing sensitivity to the impact of discrimination and oppression on the lives and experiences of older gay men and lesbian women, not only in the past but also in the present and in the future. A commitment to developing inclusive models of practice and research which allow individuals to have a voice in defining knowledge about them is also essential, as practising in an anti-oppressive way requires us to value difference rather than deny it.

This also links into anti-oppressive practice and the need for reflexivity which

> *demands that workers continually consider the ways in which their own social identity and values affect the information they gather.*

(Burke and Harrison, 2002, p231)

This may be particularly pertinent when working with 'invisible' minority groups, who unless agencies start to identify and work with, will remain 'hidden'. Individuals may not identify themselves due to concerns of being discriminated against further, and there may always be a silent minority.

ACTIVITIES

1. Consider the policy and practice of the agency you work in with regards to meeting the needs of older lesbians and gay men.

2. What implications might the Single Assessment Process have for older lesbians and gay men?

3. This chapter has explored the experiences of older lesbians and gay men. Now select a different minority group and explore how its members are marginalised and excluded by society. For example you could chose to explore older people from ethnic minorities, people with alcohol-related problems, or people with disabilities.

Other suggested reading:

> **Age Concern**, *Planning for later life as a lesbian, gay man, bisexual or transgendered person*, Age Concern England, Information Sheet LC/8, 2003.

Chapter 9

Eclectic models in working with learning disabled people – an overview of some key issues concerning health and wellness

Chris Willetts, Marilyn Essex, Andy Philpott, Sheeran Zsigo and Joanna Assey

INTRODUCTION

This chapter explores some of the challenges to 'ordinary' living experienced by people with learning disability. This is a numerically small group of people, but they have a diverse and profoundly affecting range of support needs. It is argued that many people with a learning disability experience challenges in achieving wellness and a full sense of citizenship enjoyed by many of their non-disabled peers. Meeting these needs is a large undertaking, and this chapter aims to provide an overview for readers who may be relatively new to the field of learning disabilities, but relatively experienced as practitioners and managers.

This chapter defines what learning disability is, and the historical and social policy context and the models on which current practice is based. One key challenge is that many people with a learning disability have unmet and even unrecognised needs. The purpose of this chapter is to help readers gain a better understanding of what these needs may be, and proposes how to work eclectically to address these at the micro and macro levels. People with a learning disability can be met in all walks of life, therefore it is incumbent on all care professionals to be familiar with this group of people and issues that may impact on them.

Terminology

The term 'learning disability' has been used since the early 1990s to define this 'client' group (Northfield, 2003). Before then, the terms 'mental sub-normality', 'mental retardation' and 'mental handicap' had been used. Today, these terms can appear derogatory.

Thompson (2003) argues that attention to labels and language is a major plank in anti-discriminatory practice. There is also confusion as the terms 'learning disability' and 'learning difficultly' are sometimes used interchangeably to describe the same client group.

There seems to be some confusion about whether the term learning difficulty applies to specific learning problems such as dyslexia, or to people who have more pervasive disabilities of learning which may affect global functioning. Even so, the term learning disability is not universally supported, many people given the label of learning disability prefer the label learning difficulty: (e.g. Emerson et al., 2005) This leaves a dilemma: should the term in common professional parlance (learning disability) be used, or should we use a term preferred by many to whom such labels are applied, using their preferred term learning difficulties? Others (The World Health Organisation) use the term 'intellectual disability'. Cautiously the authors have adopted the term learning disability but would support any official shift of the term to reflect what service users themselves might want.

What is learning disability?

Gates (2003) suggests that, historically, there have been different ways of defining learning disability. However, they are controversial and contested. The different ways of defining learning disability have included:

1. Legal concepts of learning disability.

2. A medical concept of learning disability.

3. Functional concepts of learning disability.

4. An anthropological view.

5. A social model of learning disability.

1. Legal concepts of learning disability

The Mental Deficiency Act of 1913 (described in Atherton, 2003) contains criteria whereby individuals could be legally classified as 'mentally defective'. The umbrella term Mental Deficiency consisted of four categories of deficiency: 'idiots', 'imbeciles', 'feeble-minded' and 'moral defectives'. The application of these criteria depended on intelligence quotient (IQ) scores. People who were deemed to have one of these Mental Deficiencies were brought within the system set up to care for this group of people, and were often detained compulsorily.

Similar legal attempts to define 'retardation' that was of such magnitude or consequence that the welfare of the individual or others was deemed to be at risk, were contained in later Mental Health legislation, i.e. Mental Health Acts of 1959 and 1983. In Section 1 of the 1983 Act, Mental Impairment is legally defined as

a state of arrested/incomplete development of mind including impairment of intelligence, social functioning and associated with abnormally aggressive or seriously irresponsible conduct.

Fulfilment of this category of mental impairment could again lead to compulsory d̲ for assessment and treatment. However, the construction and interpretation of any legal definition of learning disability is invariably fraught with theoretical and practical difficulties: a fine line between protection of society and of the individual needs to be negotiated.

2. A medical concept of learning disability

Brechin et al. (1980, cited in Gates, 2003) and Mackenzie (2005) use a medical discourse to define learning disability, which treats it as a problem that can be addressed though medical/nursing intervention. In this model, disabling medical conditions, including the genetic or chromosomal basis for many of them in the form of 'syndromes', are described and categorised, examples of this approach include Watson (2003, cited in Gates, 2003, pp22–32) or Mackenzie, 2005.

Watson claims that this approach has merit in the prevention of the causes that may lead to someone developing brain injury and damage through improved pre-conceptual, ante, peri and post natal care. She also argues that there is value in understanding the biomedical profile of someone with a learning disability, for example people who were born with Down's syndrome may often mouth breathe because of physiological differences in their nose and facial structure. Therefore carers supporting someone with this genetic inheritance may anticipate and attempt to prevent frequent chest infections that may occur because of mouth breathing. However, as Watson herself acknowledges

Simply slotting someone into categories that inform treatment or aid prognosis should be avoided if we are truly to work with people in an individual and holistic manner.

(Watson, 2003, cited in Gates 2003:22)

3. Functional concepts of learning disability

Many attempts to define learning disability have focused on psychological, educational or adaptive explanations. Such attempts depend, according to Gates (2003), on measures of educational ability or attainment, using intelligence testing (IQ), assessing psychological functioning for deviations from statistical and social norms, or by defining learning disability in terms of the person's ability to perform the adaptive skills of living (American Association of Mental Retardation, AAMR 2002). Some of the recent definitions of learning disability reflect some, or all of these functional concepts. The American Association of Mental Retardation (AAMR 2002), who still use the term retardation, which seems not to have attracted the same negative connotations as in the UK, define mental retardation as

a disability characterized by significant limitations both in intellectual functioning and in adaptive behaviour as expressed in conceptual, social, and practical adaptive skills.

Even the most recent UK government White Paper on Learning Disability (*Valuing People*, Department of Health, 2001a,14) takes a functional perspective to learning disability, which is said to include the presence of:

significant deficit in understanding new or complex information in learning new skills (impaired intelligence), reduced ability to cope independently (social impairment), it started before adulthood and has a lasting effect on development.

They do also acknowledge within their definition

> *that people with a learning disability are people first and foremost, with emphasis on what they can do (supported), rather than what they cannot do.*

However, functional concepts of learning disability have been highly significant in shaping educational and support services for people with a learning disability, recognising that they may need educational help and support with developing essential life skills.

4. An anthropological view

Edgerton (1975, cited in Begab and Richardson, 1975, p139) argues that we adopt a cultural anthropological view of learning disability. He argues that learning disability is a socially defined and constructed phenomenon. The words we use to label people and the concepts we use to define learning disability are part of that construction process. To illustrate, when considering 'adaptation' and 'social functioning', it is the 'non disabled' who define adaptation and coping by our standards and expectations: the concept of 'independence' is a non disabled perspective (Barnes et al., 1999, Swain et al., 2004).

This view emphasises the need to explore the lived experience of people with disabilities, from their own viewpoint. Recently Paul Abberley (1987), Iris Young (1990), Christopher Nolan (1999) and Mark Haddon (2004) sought to explore the 'lived' experience of disability. As Edgerton says

> *most of us... are sometimes guilty of writing (and perhaps believing) that the mentally retarded and their lives are simpler than they really are,*
>
> (Edgerton,1975, cited in Begab and Richardson, 1975:139).

Simplistic constructions of disability may be equally guilty of this if we use a non disabled perspective to define disability. The first large scale survey of adults with a learning disability in the UK (Emerson et al., 2005) attempts to enable learning disabled people to define their own experiences as people and citizens.

5. A social model of learning disability

The last 20 years has been characterised by an emergent acknowledgment of a new paradigm for understanding disability. In this view, disability is not a condition of the individual. The experience of disability is of the social restrictions in the world around them (of which the physical barriers are just a part) and not the experience of having a handicapping condition (Swain et al., 2004, p1). Therefore, the individual's experience of being disabled is created or reinforced in each encounter with disabling barriers, and that experience is often an experience of oppression (Gilbert, 1993; Hughes, 1998).

Finkelstein (1981, cited in Swain et al., 1993, p17) argued that if

> *the physical and social world were adapted for wheelchair users, 'able bodied' people would become disabled.*

Finklelstein argues that it may be society's increasing complexity which has disabled anyone who does not meet the rigid expectations of advanced industrial capitalism, technologisation and urbanisation. Oliver (1996, cited in Thompson 1997, p107) argues that

> disabled people have ... been denied inclusion into their society because of the existence of disabling barriers.

According to Swain et al., 2004, p1, these barriers may include the following.

- Physical barriers which may include building design and transport.

- Negative and demeaning attitudes by others.

- Organisations and institutions, paradoxically including education, health and social care agencies, many of which represent paternalistic, unresponsive and bureaucratic institutions.

- Language and culture which may exclude and oppress, for example the absence of disabled role models in the media, the low profile and ghettoisation of disabled people and the disability agenda in the media.

- The unequal power relationships that exist which result in disabled people being marginalised, powerless and without a strong voice at both local and national decision making levels, although some very modest moves have been made in this direction, e.g. the new Learning Disabilities Tsar (DoH, 2005b).

The discrimination experienced by many learning disabled people has been widely documented (e.g. DoH, 2001a; Learning Disabilities Taskforce, 2004; Cabinet Office, 2005; Emerson et al., 2005). According to this perspective, supporting people with intellectual or other disabilities is not just about providing individual support to service users, it is also about the social transformation that may be required so that barriers to inclusion are challenged.

These diverse definitions do not sit easily with each other. The medical and social action models appear to be in some tension, especially in the view of some (Hughes, 1998 and Thompson, 2001) that the medicalisation of disability has contributed one of the more oppressive discourses to defining the identity and experience of learning disabled people. However, there is clear evidence that learning disabled people experience higher rates of morbidity and mortality arising with their disability, but compounded by their experience of unequal and inadequate access to mainstream quality health care (DOH, 2001a; MENCAP, 2004; DoH Valuing People Support Team, 2005a; SCIE, 2006).

This theme is expanded later, but this plurality of ways of defining learning disability often generates different models and modes of working with service users, and it is argued that an eclectic model offers a synergistic model to meet apparent tensions between differing models of support for learning disabled people.

Numbers of people with a learning disability

Given that it there is no agreed way to define learning disability, it is difficult to know the precise number of people in the UK who could be classed as having a learning disability. A particular issue is that some may have borderline intellectual or learning problems yet these intellectual problems may go unrecognised or are overshadowed, for example the number of people with unrecognised borderline intellectual problems in the criminal justice system (Myers, 2004; Dyslexia Institute, 2005; Disability Rights Commission, 2005, p6).

The Foundation for People with Learning Disabilities (2004) estimates that in the UK there are between 580,000–1,750,000 people who have mild learning disabilities and a further 230,000–350,000 people have severe learning disabilities. A slightly different figure comes from the Department of Health (2001a, p14): 1,200,000 children and adults are said to have mild or moderate learning disabilities, with a further 210,000 children and adults who have a severe or profound learning disability. However these figures may not be accurate as any figure will depend on the selection and application of the criteria used, and assumes that all people with difficulties have been detected. Whatever figure is adopted, the Department of Health (2001a, p14) predicts that future numbers of people with learning disability may increase by one per cent per annum for the next 15 years. This increase is due to increased life expectancy, and a sharp rise in children diagnosed with autistic spectrum disorders, some of whom will have learning disabilities.

Although in some respects this may still numerically represent a small group of people, it represents a group of people who may have far reaching and diverse support needs if they are to be enabled to fulfil their birthright as full citizens in society.

History of learning disability services

In order to avoid neuro-linguistic gymnastics and to enable clarity, descriptive terminology used during the period being discussed will be applied, although to a modern reader these terms may be offensive.

Throughout history, disabled people have been held at all points on the spectrum from deification to detestation (Kurtz, 1981, cited in Brechin, 1981; Wolfensberger, 1992, cited in Race, 2002). More often, societies have tended to hold them closer to the latter than the former. From pre-industrial times care was aimed predominantly at protection of, and isolation from, the public. People with learning disabilities were later seen as incapable of owning or maintaining agricultural land and then like other categories of disabled people, as unproductive members in an industrial age (Finkelstein, 1990; Richardson, 2005). However during medieval times it appears that people with learning disabilities were often tolerated as village idiots and may have been able to earn some kind of living (Atherton, 2003).

During the nineteenth century people with learning disabilities came to be seen as a threat to society. They were regarded as a financial burden and the lack of inhibitions displayed by some people with a learning disability was seen as promoting socially deviant behaviour in a society committed to high moral standards (Kurtz, 1981, cited in Brechin, 1981; Gelb, 1995). It was around this time that the idea of controlling such behaviour via Eugenics was first described by Galton in 1883. He reasoned that the only way to prevent the degeneration of society was by inhibiting procreation amongst the socially deviant classes. This took the form of *institutionalisation* of the feeble-minded, the insane, those with epilepsy, alcoholism, criminality and pauperism who were all considered a threat to the stability of society (Tredgold, 1909). However, the decision to set up institutions in this country can be contrasted with the policy of mass genocide favoured in Germany and compulsory sterilisation favoured in Scandinavia in the twentieth century (Atherton, 2003).

While the large institutions, often located on the periphery of major conurbations, slowly degenerated into settings of incarceration, their original intention was to bring the disabled population to a productive level. Programmes of training to deliver basic level agricultural workers (men) and diligent domestic servants (women) formed an essential component of service delivery. At the beginning at least, many of these institutions were places of aspiration and not avoidance (Wright and Digby, 1996).

By the beginning of the twentieth century the Mental Deficiency Act of 1913 sought to provide a legal basis whereby individuals who represented a threat to society could be detained in an institution. The Wood Committee's report of 1929 aimed to examine the education of 'mental defectives' and recommended the immediate institutionalisation of 100,000 people deemed to be mentally defective. (Atherton, 2003).

Institutions

The first institutions (or asylums) set up in the early twentieth century were concerned with containment rather than rehabilitation, care or support, and catered for children and adults. These isolated 'Colonies' needed to be as self-sufficient as possible and provided accommodation, leisure and work on site for inmates. The term Colony was replaced with the implementation of the NHS Act in 1946 when the management of such institutions transferred to Regional Hospital Boards and they were renamed hospitals. Men and women were housed separately in large single sex wards to reduce the risk of heterosexual activity and thereby procreation. Inmates were required to work within the hospital, but received only token payment for their labour. Individuals were usually admitted to the hospital following medical approval, following a request from a family member who may have been unable to cope with their care at home (during a time when there was rarely any other form of support available to families).

Although for many the institutional regime was characterised by very basic living conditions, forced labour, punishment, a loss of individuality, degradation and abuse, many people formed and maintained enduring nourishing friendships with other inmates, and with some of the staff who cared for them (Deacon, 1974). For family members the lack of any alternative support often led to difficult decisions and to consequent feelings of guilt and family breakdown.

Normalisation

By the second third of the twentieth century it was becoming less acceptable to segregate disabled people from society. There was a shift away from the idea that the problem was the person's disability and an increasing realisation that environments may actually be handicapping to people. By 1959 changing social attitudes and a more liberal political agenda had paved the way for the new Mental Health Act which ended compulsory certification, so that those who were formerly detained might now be discharged back to the community. The Ely Hospital enquiry (amongst others) in the late 1960s publicised the

squalid living conditions, lack of privacy and custodial care of inmates in the mental sub-normality hospitals. This proved damning for the nursing profession and also the government of the day as the deficiencies revealed had been well known to civil servants in the Department of Health (Crossman, 1977).

The publication, in 1971 of the White Paper, Better Services for the Mentally Handicapped advocated a 50 per cent reduction in hospital places by 1991 and a corresponding increase in alternative forms of care (local authority based residential and day care). It is contestable if the transference from NHS hospital care to other forms of staffed residential care from this policy would achieve a greater level of social inclusion. This was followed in 1979 by the Jay report which recommended a philosophy of care later recognised as the principles of Normalisation.

Normalisation was a concept developed in Scandinavia and the North American continent throughout the 1950s, 60s and 70s. It is a philosophy which, its supporters claim, should be used to shape services for devalued people such as people with mental illness and learning disabilities (Nirje, 1969; Bank-Mikkelson, 1979). The origins of this philosophy can be traced to the raised awareness of human rights following the widespread abuse of human rights during the Second World War, and the inhumane treatment meted out to the inmates of the long stay institutions (Barton, 1959; Goffman, 1961). Wolfensberger developed this approach further throughout the 1970s and 1980s, and advocated the use of this approach in all human services (Wolfensberger, 1972).

Nirje (1969) defined normalisation as the making available to the 'mentally retarded' (and 'mentally ill') patterns and conditions of everyday life which are as close as possible to the norms and patterns of the mainstream of society. An ordinary life includes a normal rhythm of days, weeks and years, normal-sized living units, adequate privacy, normal access to social, emotional and sexual relationships with others, normal growing up experiences, the possibility of decently paid work, choice and participation in decisions affecting one's work.

There was some criticism of the approach arising from misunderstandings over the use and meaning of the words 'normal' and 'ordinary': what is ordinary and normal is difficult to define and this approach could end as another attempt to impose certain lifestyles on users of a service. There were examples of the rigid and zealous misapplication of normalisation, which ran counter to the spirit of the philosophy (Mesibov, 1990; Gilbert, 1993). Other critics of normalisation (Oliver, 1990; Gilbert, 1993; Barnes et al., 1999) focused on the continued professional domination of lifestyle choice, the denial of the experience of disabling barriers as a component in the lives of people themselves, and a tendency toward the imposition of a 'normalcy' onto people according to paternalistically defined cultural norms.

As a result of these types of criticism, Wolfensberger redefined normalisation as Social Role Valorization (Wolfensberger, 1983; Wolfensberger and Thomas, 1983). This was an attempt to replace the concept of 'normality' and to focus on the real goal of services, which was to restore or add the positive social value which devalued people had been deprived of or denied.

Again more recently, John O'Brien (1988) has developed this thinking in an approach often referred to as the five service accomplishments. O'Brien suggests that these should be the goals which service providers should be striving to achieve. Rather than being just a set of goals, these accomplishments can also be used as a quality assurance tool to determine the extent to which each of them is being met by a service.

The five service accomplishments – John O'Brien (1988)

1. **Presence**: this is the extent to which an individual is able and encouraged to use resources and facilities used by the rest of the local community.

2. **Participation**: clients should not only have a visible presence in their local community but should be active within it, through participation in some of the various social activities enjoyed by the rest of the local population, in effect to be citizens.

3. **Respect**: this is the extent to which clients are afforded respect and dignity, or given opportunities to gain it through achievement. The offering of first rate or high quality service is an example of the recognition of this accomplishment.

4. **Choice**: this is the offering of a broad range of real choices to clients, beyond 'a take it or leave it' approach, which for people with few options is no choice at all. Instead, a variety of realistic choices should routinely be offered although some service users who have been long-term recipients of devaluing service may have lost confidence in their own decision making or that their choices will be respected.

5. **Competence**: this is the commitment of practitioners to teach meaningful skills to clients, so that they may develop the competence to become full citizens wherever possible, but which will also enhance other people's views of them. Assertiveness, self-care and other social skills are examples of the personal competencies which will help restore value to the client, not just in their own eyes but in the view of others.

O'Brien's framework has been used widely, but the real value of this approach is that it leaves scope for creativity and inventiveness in the way in which these service accomplishments are achieved, as well as the scope for the inclusion of service users in making these sorts of decisions.

During these years other research by luminaries such as Kushlik (1970), Townsend (1973), Oswin (1978), and new exposés such as *Silent Minority* (Granada Television, 1980) maintained a momentum of support to newer models of care.

Community care to the present day

In 1989 the White Paper *Caring for People* confirmed the then government's commitment to a move from centralist services to locally based health and social care provision, with further reduction in isolated institutional care. A central aim of the following NHS and Community Care Act, (1990) was to provide the necessary support structures to enable people to remain living in their homes, should they wish to do so. Services emphasised support for informal or family carers through respite, day and domiciliary care. Central to the Act was the arrangement of individually tailored packages of care, based on an assessment of need and organised and funded by local authorities. More recently further policy and legislation has sought to improve services, emphasise inclusion and protect the rights of people with learning disabilities, these include *Moving into the Mainstream* and *Signpost for Success*, (DoH, 1998) and *Once a Day*, (DoH, 1999a). The implementation of the Disability Discrimination Act, 1995, the Human Rights Act, 1998 and the Mental Capacity Act, 2005 also had positive implications for people with learning disabilities. How these revisions might be adequately funded in the absence of personally generated income has been a continuing source of contention.

The most significant policy guidance of recent years has undoubtedly been *Valuing People*, (DoH, 2001a). While it may be argued that it was one of the longest gestations on record, being published 30 years after its most recent predecessor devoted exclusively to people with a learning disability, it gave learning disabled people a short sojourn at the political centre stage. However it lacked the added authority of a national standard framework as for other population groups, e.g. mental health, children, although it has at its heart four laudable key principles – rights, choice, independence and inclusion. It has placed an emphasis on person centred planning, increased employment and a greater range of housing options for people with a learning disability as well as the development of better advocacy services, greater support for informal carers and improved access to ordinary health services.

Valuing People: Moving Forward Together (DoH, 2004a) found that whilst significant progress is being made in the areas of access to healthcare, person centred planning, and advocacy, leisure activities and social relations still tend to be largely segregated, with the majority of social activities still undertaken and friendships formed with either other people with a learning disability, paid carers or family members. The report also highlighted other potential delays in continued improvements to services for people with learning disabilities, including the persistent delay in the closure of long stay hospitals (the last two are now scheduled for closure in 2007); the continued limitation of access to valued societal roles and employment; and the continued negative attitude of society to people with learning disabilities. The nurturing of a caring community was a significant shortfall in the NHS and Community Care Act (1990). Research would suggest that people with learning disabilities are still amongst the least accepted *disabled* groups in society, (Westbrook et al., 1993) and that society's attitudes towards this group have not improved alongside the slow changes in services.

While the majority of people with learning disabilities reside with their families, (DoH, 2005c) there have been efforts to improve residential and short break provision, while initiatives such as Supporting People and Direct Payments have further broadened the range of different accommodation and support service structures and controls available to this group. *Valuing People's* emphasis on advocacy has had a positive impact on many local authorities, its requirement that each establish a Partnership Board to involve people with learning disabilities directly in the planning and development of services which affect them has forced local authorities to consider how they promote people's inclusion and what efforts they make to enable advocacy for and by this group.

However, the government's annual report on Learning Disability (DoH, 2005c) a
edges that further challenges remain. Chief among these is to continue to
services and inclusion in planning, particularly for people with profound and multiple
abilities and those from ethnic minorities. Also a target for the year ahead is to continue
to progress work on the health inequalities still endured by people with a learning disability and improved employment opportunities to give access to paid work or valued
occupation at or above the national minimum wage.

The implementation of *Valuing People* continues to be monitored by the National Valuing
People Support Team (this role will be taken over by the Care Services Improvement
Partnership from April 2006). The aspirations of *Valuing People* have been met with enthu-
siasm by people with learning disabilities, their families and advocates. What had been
awaited was a national champion, a politically involved driver, to activate central and local
government so that these aspirations might be realised. In late 2005, the government
announced the first ever 'Tsar' for learning disabilities (DoH, 2005b). There have been
'Tsars' before in other fields, e.g. drugs, but tending to originate from the professional
workforce. The first learning disabilities 'Tsar' is a person who has learning disabilities, a
fine testimony to the many years of active self advocacy and an example from which other
spheres of society need to learn.

Different models of intervention

However, in the current provision of learning disability services, there is still a range of differing approaches which reflect the diversity of models for defining learning disability
described earlier. For example, Kay (Kay 2003, cited in Marwick and Parrish, 2003) has
attempted to map out these differing approaches to learning disability services.

Models for understanding learning disability services

(Kay, 2003, cited in Marwick and Parrish, 2003)

1. **Medical model.** 'Custodial' and medicalised approach to caring for and treating people
   with a learning disability. Care delivered by nurses and under the supervision of medical
   practitioners (psychiatrists), often in NHS settings. However, the criticism is that this
   approach can be paternalistic, reducing the experience of disabled people down to
   questions of illness, sickness and abnormality.

2. **Behavioural model.** Change in emphasis where some people with learning disability
   were seen to have maladaptive or inappropriate behaviours, that could be treated by
   behavioural psychology to 'eradicate' problem behaviours, to be replaced by more
   socially 'appropriate' behaviours. However, the emphasis may be on securing conform-
   ity to dominant social norms, inappropriate in that not all people with learning
   disability have challenging behaviour and indeed, challenging behaviour may often be a
   consequence of their experiences in impoverished care settings.

3. **Educational model.** Sees learning disability as a deficit in learning, in that people with
   learning disability may lack the skills, particularly the social and life skills, to cope with a

range of situations, making it difficult to adapt to life situations. Education and training may be the key to providing people with the essential skills for these challenges in life.

4. **Social model.** Many challenges for disabled people are the social handicaps that society places in the way of disabled people. Therefore, a key to support may be in social change to promote a more equitable and socially inclusive place for all. The rights of people are seen to be important rather than just the power, knowledge and expertise of professionals to impose help: the model of support is one of partnership.

5. **Eclectic model.** A more balanced model where it is recognised that no one model is adequate alone, but a combination of approaches may be the best approach pragmatically and philosophically.

Given the diverse range of needs that people with learning disability may have the eclectic approach may have some merit. This could be true for example when it comes to meeting education and training needs: such support could be offered adapting a more empowering partnership approach rather than using paternalistic 'professional knows best' models. Indeed Boxall (2002) and Race (2002) suggest that it may not be an 'either-or' in terms of adopting either an individualised approach or taking a social model approach: it might be a combination but driven and originating out of the aspirations and articulated needs of the learning disabled population themselves. Such an eclectic approach recognises that self determination requires educational, social and health care support provided by experts in support, but in partnership with the actual experts on learning disability, the service users themselves. Perhaps the most important and complex challenge is about how we effectively tap into that expertise, and enable learning disabled people to 'speak' and be heard, (Walmsley and Johnson, 2005).

Kay sums up the need for services to reflect a shift in power from a professional centred model to a service user centred model, coupled with a shift from an ethics and duty model to a 'rights' model, where quality support is an entitlement and is offered in partnership which celebrates the equal status and valid perspective of the user of the service (Kay 2003, cited in Marwick and Parrish, 2003).

Person Centred Planning

This value base can be turned into actual practice with learning disabled people through a Person Centred Planning process.

A person-centred approach to planning support means it should start with the individual (not with services), and take account of their wishes and aspirations (Thomas and Woods, 2003; Mansell and Beadle-Brown, 2005). Person Centred Plans (PCPs) are a mechanism for reflecting the needs and preferences of a person with a learning disability and cover such issues as housing, education, employment and leisure (DOH, 2001a, p49). PCPs are not intended to replace the integrated care approach or community care assessments or care plans which are required by legislation (NHS and Community Care Act, 1990) but to inform and enhance all other assessments and reviews. PCPs are not concerned with the allocation of resources or eligibility criteria as other plans may need to be.

PCP is a fundamentally different way of seeing and working with individuals. This is achieved by discovering and acting on what is important to a person, and gives a structure to continue to listen and learn about what is important to a person now and in the future, and includes family and friends. It requires a fundamental shift in thinking from a 'power over' relationship to a 'power with' relationship. PCP is a basis for problem-solving and negotiation to access the resources necessary to pursue the person's aspirations. The process should be a positive experience by which people can record their aims and ambitions as well as the support they need to help them reach their goals. The focus should be on people achieving the lives they want rather than the production of a plan for the sake of having one.

Key features of PCP

PCP contains key features which distinguish it from other forms of care planning (DoH, 2001a):

- The person is at the centre.
- Family members and friends are full partners, (placing people in the context of their family and community).
- A PCP reflects a person's abilities (rather than disabilities). Services are delivered in the context of the life a person chooses rather than their lifestyle being dictated by existing or available services.
- PCP builds a shared commitment to action that recognises a person's rights, an ongoing process of working together to maintain and improve quality of life.
- PCP leads to continual listening, learning and action and helps a person get what they want from life.

PCP is not a means to an end in itself, to be effective it must result in real change for people with learning disabilities. It is a key element to achieving delivery of the government's objectives outlined in *Valuing People*, (DoH, 2001a).

Some different approaches to Person Centred Planning

Any planning approach which embodies the key features described above could be described as Person Centred Planning, and different forms of PCP have been developed (Brewster and Ramcharan, 2005).

1. Essential lifestyle planning
Developed by Smull and Burke-Harrison (1992, cited in Brewster and Ramcharan 2005). It aims to be a snapshot of how someone wants to live today, serving as a blueprint for how to support someone tomorrow. It should communicate what is important to someone using a user-friendly format, it is a way of making sure that the person is heard, regardless of the severity of his or her disability. The best ELPs reflect the balances between competing desires, needs, choice and safety. It does this by considering the perspectives of those who know and care about the person, including what they like and admire about the person and their thoughts about what might constitute a good day and a bad day for the

person. This is a particularly useful tool for people with profound disabilities who may find communication difficult or where there is confusion about how to keep someone healthy or safe. It focuses on the immediate needs.

2. PATH

PATH was developed by O'Brien et al. (1993). It focuses on a desirable future or dream and the steps needed to work towards this. It is a way of planning direct and immediate action towards future aspirations. It tends to be a more graphical illustration of the person's dreams and the support needed to work towards them. This is a useful tool for people who have some sense of a better future, but need help to describe it and plan the steps or support necessary to achieve their goal, or where people feel they have little to look forward to.

3. MAP

MAP was developed by Falvey et al. (1997). It retells a person's story to remind us who they are, their gifts and dreams. It also outlines the nightmares we are working to avoid. It leads to goal-setting, action plans and enlists the help of people who can make it happen. It is particularly useful for avoiding the repetition of past mistakes.

4. Personal futures planning

Developed by Mount and Zwernik in 1988, it involves a committed group of people who describe what a person's life looks like now and looks at what they would like for the future. It is useful to help learn more about a person's life (unlike PATH, which assumes knowledge) and create a vision for the future. It aims to promote changes in existing services where these are unhelpful to the individual.

However, in dealing with individuals it will be clear that one format may be more suitable than another. PCP is about creativity and being guided by the person whose plan is being developed therefore it would be inappropriate to prescribe the format to be used.

The facilitation of Person Centred Planning

Many people with learning disabilities may require assistance to develop a PCP and the careful choice of a facilitator will do much to influence the accuracy and success of the plan. A facilitator should be someone who knows the person well and is able to support them in recording their plan in a way that is meaningful for them. Anyone can facilitate a person centred plan, however typically they would be facilitated either by the service user themselves, a carer or friend, a nurse or social worker, keyworker, advocate or an employer. A plan is not an outcome, person centred planning is an ongoing process, once developed a plan needs to record changes in the person's life as they occur and ensure that all those involved continue to work towards the goals recorded there.

The PCP process

Valuing People (DoH, 2001a) identified groups who would be a priority for Person Centred Planning, but by now many people with a learning disability should have had the process explained to them and been offered the opportunity to complete a plan. The Valuing

People Support Team (2004, p4) continue to emphasise the value of person centred planning for all people with a learning disability.

Although several differing approaches to PCP have been described here it is important to bear in mind that it is the process which is important rather than the format. However there are some elements which should be considered or included in a good person centred plan. These include (Thomas and Woods, 2003, p159):

- Who to involve?

- Who am I?

- What matters to me?

- Support I need for these to happen.

- Understanding my communication.

- Support I need to stay healthy and safe.

- What questions need to be answered?

- Is there anything which has not been covered?

- What needs to happen now?

- How can we keep the plan alive?

It is clear that while person centred plans will differ according to the personality, needs and nature of the person involved, certain standards should still be maintained. These may include that (Brewster and Ramcharan, 2005):

- The person themselves chose who to involve.

- They chose where to plan (comfortable surroundings).

- They chose when to plan (convenient and appropriate times).

- The plan should always reflect the individual person rather than their disability or concentrating only on needs.

- The plan should be owned (and where possible kept) by the person themselves.

- Making a plan should not be the end result. It needs to be seen as really happening for the person and as a force for changing people's lives for the better.

- The plan should aim to be a positive picture and where it needs to include information about keeping healthy and safe etc, these must be recorded in a respectful way.

Valuing People (DoH 2001a) also stressed that there must be a link between Person Centred Plans and vocational plans (led by Connexions for young people), health action plans (steered by an identified health professional), housing plans (including a joint housing/community care assessment) and communications plans (where the person has communications difficulties). However, Mansell and Beadle-Brown (2005) argue that PCPs might carry more weight if they had legal weight, and more use was made of Direct Payments and Independent Living Trusts and that performance management of learning disability services was based on quality not quantity!

Now the issue of the health of learning disabled people will be considered in order to explore how an eclectic approach may reconcile the different approaches and models of support, a synergy which may be achieved through PCPs in the form of Health Action Plans, and Health Facilitation which attempts to address the barriers to accessing health support, an integrated approach which marries an individual approach with a social approach to the issue.

The health of people with a learning disability

People who have a learning disability suffer increased health related problems compared to the general population (Acheson, 1998; Barr et al., 1999; NHS Scottish Executive, 2004; DoH 2001a, DoH, 2005a).

Some examples: coronary heart disease (CHD) is the second most common cause of death for the general population in the UK and is the same in the learning disabled population (Hollins et al., 1998), although rates of CHD in learning disabled people are increasing due to increased longevity and lifestyle changes associated with community living (Carter and Jancar, 1983; Turner and Moss, 1996; Wells et al., 1995). Respiratory disease is the leading cause of death for people with intellectual disabilities (Carter and Jancar, 1983; Hollins et al., 1998; Puri et al., 1995), much higher than for the general population.

Prevalence rates for schizophrenia in people with learning disabilities are approximately three times greater than for the general population (Doody et al., 1998), with higher prevalence rates for South Asian adults with intellectual disabilities compared to White adults with intellectual disabilities (Chaplin et al., 1996). People with co-existing mental health problems and learning disabilities are at risk of receiving no mental health service, due to the lack of communication between mainstream psychiatry services and intellectual disability psychiatry services (Hassiotis et al., 2000; Moss et al., 1996; Roy et al., 1997).

A very high proportion of people with intellectual disabilities are receiving prescribed psychotropic medication, most commonly anti-psychotic medication (Branford, 1994; Clarke et al., 1990; Robertson et al., 2000b). Anti-psychotics are most commonly prescribed for challenging behaviours rather than schizophrenia, despite no evidence for their effectiveness in treating challenging behaviours and considerable evidence of harmful side-effects (Emerson, 2001).

Women with intellectual disabilities are much less likely to engage in breast cancer examinations or receive invitations to mammography than the general population (Davies and Duff, 2001; Piachaud and Rohde, 1998; Djuretic et al. 1999), despite a 90 per cent attendance rate at mammography clinics when invited (Davies and Duff, 2001).

The poor health chances of this population have been frequently identified elsewhere in the literature (e.g. Mencap, 2004; DoH 2005a; Emerson et al., 2005). However, many of these individual health problems experienced by learning disabled people are compounded by problems with access to quality mainstream services, where they may not receive proper and appropriate support with those health needs (DoH, 2001a; Mencap, 2004; Learning Disability Taskforce, 2004, Emerson et al. 2005). This neatly illustrates again the fact that learning disabled people may require an eclectic response in that despite having needs requiring support from health services and individual practitioners, it is equally the lack of inclusion and access highlighted by the social model of disability which may be a critical factor in whether these services are received.

Public health, health promotion and health improvement in the field of learning disabilities

Public health and health promotion strategies are key concepts in ensuring that people who have a learning disability enjoy the fullest benefits of citizenship and enjoy the greatest sense of personal wellbeing and health (DoH, 2001a, 2001b, 2002).

Public health
Public health aims to reduce disease and health inequalities (Faculty of Public Health Medicine of the Royal Colleges of Physicians of the United Kingdom, 2001) and is a strategy of change and improvement which may be directed to disadvantaged populations, such as people with learning disability. However, there is a risk that the lack of access to health might not get attributed to wider structural policy making and political structures (Laverack, 2004) but service users themselves might be 'blamed' for not taking up services. Some service users might see their health problems as inevitable consequences of their 'disabling condition' impacting on their psychological wellbeing. This may be of great significance to the learning disabled person given that this population have historically been disadvantaged through institutional and narrowly medically orientated care provision and societal oppression (Laverack, 2004).

The shifts from institutionalised care to community care (Jones, 1999; DoH, 2001a) are one attempt to redress this imbalance, but this move has not always improved the quality of life for this population, with conflicting evidence of the impact of deinstitutionalisation on health (Finkelstein and French, 1993; Straus and Kastner, 1996; Conroy and Adler, 1998; Hayden, 1998). A further example of marginalisation of the learning disabled health agenda comes with public health policy aimed towards the needs of the general population; the specific needs of the learning disabled population could be clouded by the dramatic needs associated with cancers, smoking and alcohol. However, it is noted that although people who have a learning disability partake very little in smoking and alcohol they are generally 'unfit' and have sedentary lifestyles that predispose them to coronary heart disease (Beange, 1996).

Therefore whilst learning disabled people can benefit from public health initiatives, there is still little recognition that they are a population that may require a more inclusive public health agenda, particularly one concerned with challenging the social barriers to fulfilling and healthier lifestyles and options, and promoting inclusion and access to timely and appropriate health support.

Health promotion
Health promotion is also designed to improve health and wellbeing and prevent disease (Naidoo and Wills, 1998). Health education, disease prevention and health surveillance are significant components of health promotion (Tones, 2002). There is emphasis on lifestyle and living conditions or, to elaborate further, the individual's lifestyle and the structural

elements within it, such as environmental and financial factors that may contribute to 'wellness' or 'illness' (World Health Organisation, 1984).

On the other hand the DoH (1999a) highlight that health promotion programmes can inadvertently reinforce health inequalities because they may overlook the concerns of the minorities such as the learning disabled by focusing on the 'wrong' issues, or can be expressed in complex and inappropriate language (Howells, 1996; Arevalo, 2001; Lindsey, 2002; DoH, 1999b; DoH, 2006). *Choosing Health* (DoH, 2004b) however proposes a move from illness based intervention to a health and wellness focus.

Meeting individul health needs and health facilitation

An example of the synergy of an i. *ual* approach to meeting needs with a social model approach.

Supporting the global health and social needs of people who have a learning disability may require an eclectic, perhaps synergistic approach. The issue of health improvement and promoting wellbeing is a useful domain to illustrate the need for this. As said earlier, there may be some apparent tension between medical explanations of disability and the social model paradigm. However, at the same time it is recognised that people with a learning disability often have a significant morbidity and mortality associated with having a learning disability. This is compounded by the fact (again shown elsewhere in this chapter) that their health needs may often go undetected or unmet, (paradoxical given the historical dominance of the medical model in the learning disability field), coupled with the fact that learning disabled people experience difficulties in accessing timely and adequate health support from mainstream health services.

Valuing People stated that people who have a learning disability are to be assigned a health facilitator and should be registered with general practitioners with Health Action Plans (HAPs) to be in place by the year 2005 (DoH, 2001a). Further guidance on Health Action Planning and Health Facilitation (DoH, 2002) was published which emphasises best practice in Health Action Planning, but whether this will improve the health of this client group is uncertain (Gates, 2003; Fisher, 2004).

Policy and research (DoH, 2001a; Mencap, 2004; Bailey et al., 2005; Northway et al., 2005) highlight initiatives that promote equity of healthcare access for this group of people although health facilitation alone may be not without risks (Beange, 1996). Medical illness focused Health Plans, as opposed to holistic wellbeing ones that lack service user involvement, may be one unintended consequence.

Health facilitation

Matthews (2003) emphasises that carers are well placed to respond to service user needs and aspirations. Bailey et al. (2005) suggest the essential responsibilities for health facilitators are:

- identifying and recording health targets for the HAP
- supporting access to all health services including NHS screening programmes
- ensuring the HAP is an integral part of person centred planning

- helping to identify and meet health education needs
- monitoring individual health outcomes through regular review and where necessary agreeing changes to the HAP.

Assessment of health needs should be part of the PCP process (DoH, 2002) and highlights that simplicity is essential when conducting them so that wherever possible the service user is able to be involved even if they have severe intellectual difficulties. Bailey et al. (2005) recommend using a validated tool to assess health needs such as the 'OK Health Check' (Matthews and Hegarthy, 1997).

Bailey et al. (2005) suggest a framework for health assessment that pays particular attention to certain themes when conducting a health action plan and include:

- details of the need for health interventions
- oral health and dental care
- fitness and mobility
- continence
- vision
- hearing
- nutrition
- emotional needs
- medication taken and side effects
- records of any screening tests.

Guidance for completion includes questions the health facilitator may wish to consider and comprises a series of questions including medical health, what previous assessments have been carried out and by whom, what support the health facilitator may need, and how the client may perceive their health and the support they may want (Bailey et al. 2005).

Laverack (2004) suggests that in working with marginalised groups, health and social care professionals need a clear understanding and awareness of the more social dimensions to the problem:

1. Causes of marginalisation.

2. Importance of including learning disabled individuals and groups in political and social power structures.

3. Supporting marginalised groups in challenging power structures.

4. Awareness of powerlessness and its repercussions in physical, psychological and social aspects of providing services.

5. Prioritising work concerned with removing and challenging policies that create exclusion.

Northway et al. (2005) also suggest:

1. Right competencies, skills, experiences and locations to enable high quality care delivery to happen.

2. Utilisation of education sources where appropriate.

Perez (2005) also suggests some guidelines for effective consultation for general practitioners which would give people with learning disability the opportunity to best represent themselves with regard to their health, thus enabling people and encourage autonomy. There is also a need to improve the information and guidance provided for service users and carers from ethnic minority groups. Therefore, health action planning and facilitation should take place face-to-face, and must also address cultural sensitivity and diversity (Tait and Genders, 2002).

Although problems such as meeting service user's health needs and aspirations may appear to require one mode of response or approach, many of the challenges faced by someone with a learning disability may require more than one approach. Health needs may need a medical response from health service providers, but also may involve a service user needing to learn new behaviours, and new skills (reflecting psychological and educational approaches), as well as support to challenge barriers and obstacles to inclusion and access that are often socially constructed (the social model). All must be driven by a person centred approach that listens to and values the wishes, views and experiences of the learning disabled person (the anthropological perspective). An eclectic approach to providing support for people with a learning disability may very well be entirely justified.

Conclusion

This chapter has briefly explored some of the challenges to 'ordinary' living experienced by people with learning disability. It was argued that many people with a learning disability experience challenges in achieving wellness as well as achieving a full sense of citizenship enjoyed by many of their non-disabled peers. The range of definitions of learning disability and approaches adopted to support services, which largely arise out of these perspectives, were discussed together with the historical and social policy context on which current practice is often based.

One of the key challenges is that many people with a learning disability have unrecognised and unmet needs such as in the area of health and wellbeing. The fact that health challenges may often arise out of the individual's experience of their 'disabling condition' may require a medical approach yet health may also be an experience of encountering disabling barriers and exclusion. A synergistic approach to supporting learning disabled people is proposed that recognises that people may have medical, psychological and education needs, whilst the social model complements the development of support services by recognising that social barriers and exclusion need to be challenged in parallel. Above all the anthropological perspective advises us the starting point of all support should be the aspirations of the service users themselves, so that we need to find ways to help them 'speak' and be heard: an appropriate synergistic person centred framework for offering support in partnership with those we claim to be supporting.

Chapter 10

Adult protection for community care/vulnerable adults

Linda Naylor

INTRODUCTION

There has been a rapid development of work in the area of adult protection or adult abuse in the past ten years, and it now occupies a central position in any work with vulnerable adults. Despite the fact that the first government guidance to local authorities and their partners did not appear until 2000 (Department of Health, 2000), many areas were by then already well advanced in the work of protecting vulnerable adults. No Secrets in 2000 took this a stage further by requiring that all local authorities have a multi-agency policy by October 2001. As with many good initiatives, one of the main difficulties with this was the lack of any additional funds to accompany it. Many multi-agency policies are led strongly by one agency, with the others showing less commitment. This is gradually being improved by the appointments of Adult Protection Co-ordinators in many areas.

In the area of child protection, there was a slow process of growing awareness. This started with recognition in the 1960s, firstly in the USA, that young babies being presented at hospitals were sometimes multiply injured at the hands of their parents. A period of intense attention to the issue of physical abuse followed. There was some parallel attention to neglect in the form of 'inadequate or problem families', although this was not always viewed as child abuse. During the 1980s, attention began to focus on the sexual abuse of children. In the late 1990s, expressions of concern prompted the refocus of services that encompassed a broader group of children in need in the assessment process. This included a greater emphasis on emotional abuse.

Adult protection has followed a similar evolutionary process. Initially, there was a lot of interest in two separate fields. Firstly, in the 1970s, the physical abuse of older people hit the headlines with such phrases as 'Granny bashing' (Baker, 1975). Formal recognition of elder abuse in Britain arose in 1993 with Department of Health guidelines (1993). In a completely separate development in the same year (Brown and Turk, 1993), the issue of the sexual abuse of adults with learning disabilities became the focus of attention. There was little recognition of the other areas of abuse until the mid 1990s when additional categories were at least noted. As with child protection, attention was focused on particular types of abuse, and the others not always acknowledged. In addition, the focus was on learning disability and older people. There was very little emphasis on the other vulnerable adult client groups:

- the physically disabled
- those with sensory loss
- those with mental health difficulties.

Although policies are now meant to cover this broader group, they still receive little attention in either practice or research.

Defining adult abuse

The first definition that is important is defining who are vulnerable adults, and who therefore fall within protective policies. DoH (2000) adopted the Law Commission definition as follows:

> *anyone of 18 years and over who is or may be in need of community care services by reason of mental or other disability, age or illness and who is or may be unable to take care of himself or herself, or unable to protect himself or herself against significant harm or serious exploitation.*

There have been some discussions about changing this definition to include those not eligible for services. The Association of the Directors of Social Services (ADSS) (2005) proposed widening the scope of policies to include safeguarding adult citizen rights.

The difficulties of defining adult abuse parallel the historical development cited. Many early definitions were specific to the abuse of older people and did not serve any wider function for other adult client groups. Terms like 'elder abuse' were not helpful in this respect. Finkelhor and Pillemer (1988) spoke of *definitional array* with no generally accepted term for elder abuse at that point. Action on Elder Abuse (1995) adopted the following definition:

> *Elder abuse is a single or repeated act or lack of appropriate action, occurring within any relationship where there is an expectation of trust, which causes harm or distress to an elder person.*

There was a gradual broadening to create a definition which included all vulnerable adult groups, culminating in the *No Secrets* definition (DoH, 2000):

> *Abuse is a violation of an individual's human and civil rights by any other person or persons.*

This definition is very broad and includes any rights issue, with no limiting factor of harm being caused. It is therefore not a functional definition which agencies can use to determine which cases to respond to as abuse, and which to investigate. As in child protection, there is a need to define the categories of abuse and thresholds for action to guide local decision-making. Often, it is not the category of abuse that challenges staff but the threshold for taking action. At what point should staff refer the matter on to Social

Services for investigation? Very few multi-agency policies discuss this issue, although some guidance by Brown and Stein (1998) suggests such factors as individual frailty, the effect of the abuse, and risk of repetition being taken into account.

Categories of abuse have again expanded as awareness has grown. Initial emphasis on the physical and financial abuse of the elderly (Lau and Kosberg, 1979) was perpetuated in most studies of older people abuse. Much of the work on learning disability emphasised sexual abuse. However, there is a real attempt in *No Secrets* to be both generic and also broad in categorisation with the use of the following categories:

- physical abuse

- sexual abuse

- psychological abuse

- financial or material abuse

- neglect and acts of omission

- discriminatory abuse.

The addition of the final category of discriminatory abuse was unexpected by most specialists in this field. This category does not appear in child protection and largely overlaps with the others. If someone is being discriminated against, this might be expected to show itself in physical or psychological abuse. However, the highlighting of discrimination reflects the *Disability Discrimination Act,* 1995 and of course the requirements of the older legislation in relation to sexual and racial discrimination (*Sex Discrimination Act,* 1975 and 1986, *Race Relations Act ,*1976).

Vulnerability and context

There are a number of factors which make certain adults vulnerable to abuse. In looking at these, it is important to remember that all these factors could be present and the contexts allow for abuse, but it needs an abuser for abuse to take place. It is not the responsibility of the vulnerable adult that they are abused. There is a danger in seeing certain groups of adults as necessarily and automatically frail and vulnerable.

One vulnerability factor is over-compliance, where vulnerable adults are used to having little say in services and accepting whatever treatment comes their way. This can lead to a lack of resistance to poor treatment or abuse. An absence of wider social networks can create isolation, leaving some people easy prey to abusers and unlikely to speak out if they are abused. Some will be dependent on their abuser for basic survival and fear retaliation. The victim may blame themselves for the abuser's behaviour or feel protective towards them. Many vulnerable adults have poor access to non-specialist services, and although they have a range of services specific to their disability, do not know how to access the police and more routine help (Williams, 1995). Many adults with learning or physical disability have limited sexual knowledge, despite attempts in recent years to counter this. Older people can also lack the confidence to describe sexual matters due to a particular generational view of the subject. Some vulnerable adults need help with their personal care which gives more people access to them and the heightened possibility of abuse. It can also make it harder for someone to be sure that it is abuse they are receiving.

Any communications limitation makes adults more vulnerable because of their limited methods of 'speaking out' if something happens to them. Sometimes, the only way for them to show something untoward has happened is by their behaviour. These behaviours can then be labelled as 'challenging' rather than recognising the cause. In both older people and people with learning disability, multiple disabilities seem to create greater vulnerability to abuse.

In Brown and Turk's research (1992):

- 60% of the victims of sexual abuse had a severe or profound learning disability and

- 40% had a mild or borderline disability.

This is particularly surprising as a proportion of this severely disabled group have no way of communicating that they have been abused and therefore would not show up in the statistics. For some vulnerable adults, particularly those with dementia, mental illness or learning disability, confusion can be blamed for disclosures, and therefore appropriate action may not be taken.

In the area of sexual abuse, there is the additional factor of the behaviour of sexual abusers and the links with the vulnerability of the adults involved. There is limited research, but it appears that some of the grooming and insidious build-up present in the sexual abuse of children is also present with adults. It is possible that such abusers pick certain groups of vulnerable adults because they will make poor witnesses in court and would have had little chance of getting into court until recent changes were made.

There has been a general assumption that a significant proportion of domestic abuse is related to carer stress. Eastman (1984) started the debate with his portrayal of the stressed daughter looking after her elderly mother. Homer and Gilleard (1990) characterised the abuser as male or female with alcohol problems. In their research, 45% of carers admitted to one form of abuse and most were spouses or children. The emphasis on 'stressed carers' has been challenged by Bennett and Kingston (1993) as promoting a *victim mentality*. The presence of disruptive behaviour in the elderly victim and the poor quality of early relationships are the strongest predictors of abuse (Biggs et al., 1995). Kappeler (1995) suggests that in a society based on exchange relationship, those with nothing to exchange for their care are more likely to be victimised.

There is an increasing interest in both the causes and the contexts of abuse. In terms of individual causes, the following factors are recognised:

- psychological causes

- drugs

- alcohol

- financial problems

- the dependency of the victim

- provocation by the victim

- stress of the carer

- social isolation (Decalmer and Glendenning, 1997)

The role that institutions can play in abuse and mistreatment is also recognised:

- long hours

- low pay and

- low prestige

were identified by Pillemer and Moore (1989).

There has been a wealth of information published about indicators, or signs and symptoms of abuse. Whilst these can lead to a false optimism about spotting abuse, when used with caution they can help workers be more aware. Some lists are category specific, although a high level of overlap is acknowledged (Breckman and Adelman, 1988). Most agencies now include such lists in their policies and they are increasingly generic rather than specific to one adult client group.

Incidence

The difficulties of defining abuse make it challenging to be clear about its incidence. Aggregate data cannot be discussed as each survey has defined abuse in a different way. Estimates will also be based on reported incidents which by no means reflect the whole position. *No Secrets* (DoH, 2000) now means that local authorities will at least attempt to monitor adult abuse statistics, although definitions and thresholds will still cause uncertainty. An Action on Elder Abuse study (2006) has added to our understanding of the reporting of incidents of abuse to local authorities with a monitoring study. Very few referrals are made by the public. The majority of the victims in this study were aged 65 or over (54.8%). The next largest group were adults with learning disability – 25.4%. Referrals came from Social Services (13.6%), Service providers (14.2%), family (4.9%) and the vulnerable adult (5.9%). The most common form of abuse was physical (33.8%) followed by neglect.

In practice and in research, the emphasis on certain categories of abuse for certain client groups means that incidence figures remain at best partial. For example, much research on the abuse of older people does not ask 'samples' about sexual abuse, assuming this not to be so relevant (Pritchard, 1990). Neglect and psychological abuse are not emphasised in any research and are more difficult to specify, whilst research into the abuse of those with mental health problems or physically disabled adults is scarce and limited.

Amongst the concern about the sexual abuse of adults with learning disability, it is easy to lose sight of the very common stories told by practitioners about the financial abuse of this group. Bewley (1997) shows how little amount of control many people with a learning disability have over their money and possessions. Assumptions that are often made (i.e. that people are incapable) means that real choice about finance is not available; there are also more extreme cases of abuse.

Incidence figures for the sexual abuse of those with learning disability are readily available.

- Doucette (1986) found that 67% of disabled women and 34% of non-disabled women experienced sexual abuse.

- Hard and Plumb (1987) stated that 58 per cent of day centre users reported sexual abuse.

The major research in this area has been by Brown, Stein and Turk (1995) who estimated that there would be 1,200 new cases of serious sexual abuse of adults with learning disability per year. Of the victims in their research, 73% were female and 27% were male, which is similar to the gender composition of the victims in Pritchard's (1992) older people study. Physical abuse was the main category of abuse type. Williams (1995) undertook broader research into crime against adults with learning disability, and particularly highlighted the effect of low level ongoing harassment and minor crimes, which leave this group too tolerant and accepting of harsh or abusive treatment. Abuse by other service users was also seen as significant.

For older people, there has been no major prevalence study in Britain. There is more extensive research in the USA, and this allows researchers to hazard guesses at British incidences. For example, Ogg and Bennett (1992) estimated that 4% of older people would be subject to abuse or inadequate care. Pritchard (1995) has undertaken extensive research in Britain and concluded that between 5 and 10% of older people suffer some form of abuse. She also highlighted the issue of stranger abuse and the vulnerability of older people to gang abuse and harassment (Pritchard, 1993). Aitken and Griffin (1996) concluded from their research that financial abuse was so common place that workers did not recognise it as an area of concern.

There is little research into the abuse of physically disabled adults. Simanowitz (1995) found that in his small sample of adults with either physical or learning disability,

- 50% had experienced violence or harassment and

- 46% had experienced psychological abuse in the past year.

Also in the past year,

- 21% had experienced physical abuse

- 14% neglect

- 10% medical abuse and

- 7% financial abuse.

There was a low response rate in this research, and perhaps those who responded were the disabled adults with the most concern about abuse. Brown et al. (1999) comment on the high rates of personal and sexual violence against deaf people both within the deaf community and at the hands of others.

For adults with mental health problems, the limited research reflects the myth perpetuated in the media that they are a risk to the public rather than being at risk in any way themselves. Survivors of child sexual abuse are twice as likely to have a current or lifetime mental health disorder. There are clear links with past child abuse and re-victimisation as adults, so there will be a clear overlap between people abused as children, mental illness symptoms and being re-abused as adults (Messman-Moore and Long, 2000). Lipschitz et al. (1996) stated that 76% of women who attended one psychiatric outpatient unit had been raped or sexually assaulted as adults in the past. Carmen (1984) said that 30% of female psychiatric inpatients had been physically abused by their male partners. Wienhardt, et al. (1999) stated that women with severe mental illness had an increased risk of being sexually coerced, and in their sample 13% of female outpatients had been forced into sex against their will in the past two months. Briere et al. (1997) found that 42% of female emergency psychiatric patients had experienced physical assaults in an adult relationship and 37% sexual assaults. There are some alarming figures about the risks to women from sexual abuse while in hospital. In one particular psychiatric institution, Nibert et al. (1989) found that 71% of in-patients had been threatened with violence, 53% physically assaulted and 38% sexually assaulted while in hospital. The intrinsic problem with assessing the level of abuse in mental health services is that what service users say is often seen as part of their condition rather than a credible account of a real experience.

There have been a number of inquiry reports into institutional abuse that are often in relation to concerns about a specific residential setting (for example, Gibbs et al., 1987). Some of these reports have emphasised the corruption factor of one individual, the 'bad apple' hypothesis, which is an inadequate explanation for abusive cultures (Wardhaugh and Wilding, 1993). Camden and Islington Community Health Services NHS Trust (1999) recommended creating an open environment with effective whistle blowing procedures. There was also an emphasis on involving residents in decision making. The Longacre Inquiry (1998) recommended the use of advocacy schemes to help to reduce abuse in institutions, but in many areas these remain very sparse. However, common themes emerge from the inquiry reports, with abuse seen as resulting from lack of staff training, professional isolation, stress, low morale, organisational culture, personal characteristics of both victims and perpetrators and a lack of adequate resources. The reluctance of clients to make complaints, and the stifling of them, mean that institutional abuse can go unrecognised. The misuse of restraint and the lack of policies around the sexuality of service users also contribute.

There have been fewer research studies devoted to institutional abuse, and the emphasis has largely been on domestic abuse. Decalmer and Glendenning (1997) suggested that the most common abuse is institutional abuse, where the environment and practices of the institution become abusive in themselves. Wardaugh and Wilding (1993) suggested that the depersonalisation of the institution allows for the viewing of individuals as less than human, which creates a climate for abuse. Pillemer and Moore's (1989) research, although dated, shows that most staff were motivated by a desire to be helpful:

- 32% of staff found the job stressful

- 36% claimed to have seen an incident of physical abuse in the past year, and

- 40% had committed at least one act of psychological abuse in the past year.

Jack (1994) suggested that there is a gender issue in institutional abuse with a predominantly female workforce abusing a mainly female population. (Stanley et al., 1999) said that many approaches to institutional abuse tend to focus on individual workers with the idea of flushing out the individual to solve the problem.

Training programmes are often used to address institutional abuse with the assumption being that increased training will prevent future abuse. Taylor and Dodd (2003) showed in their research that the effectiveness of training may be variable – 75% of the research sample had received training on abuse, but there remained a culture of acceptance of service user to user abuse which was not always taken as seriously. Staff in this study seemed to make their own judgements about reporting and 35% would only report an abuse incident if they themselves considered the abuse severe enough. Seventy five percent of staff would only report the abuse if there was concrete evidence and 20% were hesitant to report an abuse allegation that may not be true. Twenty percent were reluctant to report abuse if it were breaking the service user's confidentiality. The handling of allegations against staff was concerning with 10 % reluctant to report if the alleged perpetrator was a staff member – 30% would discuss the concerns with the staff member first, which could destroy evidence.

An additional concern is how effectively institutional abuse is investigated. The roles of the Commission for Social Care Inspection, the police and Social Services are not always clear in local policies. McCreadie (2001) set a standard that the role of the Registration and Inspection should be clear and that they should monitor any allegations from residential care. The roles of agencies in institutional abuse vary around the country and are often ad hoc and confused.

Links with other family violence

It is important to place adult abuse in the context of some related areas while not losing the emphasis that not all adult abuse happens in the home setting. There are links with domestic violence, and Finkelhor and Pillemer (1988) confirm that elder abuse is often spouse abuse. Domestic violence is most commonly viewed as male physical violence towards female partners (Johnson, 1995). Finkelhor and Pillemer (1988) say that even where the two adults are not married, there are more parallels with domestic violence than child abuse because of the rights and choices of adults and their effects. The power imbalance between two individuals allowing one to act as abuser is common to both situations, and so clearly, some of the abuse that takes place against vulnerable adults is in the form of domestic violence, (e.g. an older couple where one partner has always been violent to the other and they are now vulnerable and frail). The cycle of violence has also been recognised in some families where violent acts have been perpetrated within families, and some of it in the form of adult abuse. However, there is a danger that physical abuse is emphasised at the expense of the other categories of abuse where links are made with domestic violence.

It is necessary to remember the need to define whether victims of domestic violence are also vulnerable adults and fall within protective procedures. For example, Community Care (16 May 2000) discussed the case of a disabled woman suffering domestic violence and the appropriate response, all with no mention of vulnerable adult procedures. In *No Secrets*, (DoH, 2000) there is no mention of domestic violence despite recent guidance. This separation of the two interrelated areas is a significant shortfall in practice. Domestic violence is not always a feature of adult abuse, but the vulnerability of the adults should always be considered in domestic violence situations.

There are very significant theoretical links with child protection. Clearly, there are also huge differences – not least that adults have the rights and choices of adults, and are not protected by child care legislation which assumes children lack capacity and need protection. Despite the progressive proposals in *Who Decides?* (Lord Chancellor's Department, 1997) there is still no emergency protective legislation for adults that is equivalent to the Emergency Protection Orders in the Children Act 1989. The adult is presumed in law to have the right to make their own decisions and there are very limited powers to interfere with these.

Stevenson (1996) discusses the over-proceduralisation of child protection and the dangers of this happening in adult protection. The emphasis on risk and the desire to simplify the process of decision-making has some important lessons for adult protection. Stevenson also discusses the danger of protection being split off from wider welfare issues, which has caused the need for refocusing in child protection and could happen again in adult protection. Adult protection work needs to be set within a wider framework of needs assessment and care management.

There are other obvious learning points from Area Child Protection Committees for the new Adult Protection Committees forming as the result of *No Secrets*. Stevenson (1996) has stressed that inter-agency cooperation is just as crucial in adult protection as it is in child protection. Every child death inquiry from Maria Colwell (1974) onwards has accentuated the need for good inter-agency communication and this is as true in adult protection. The effect of *No Secrets* is limited compared with the much more prescriptive *Working Together to Safeguard Children* (DoH, 1999) and all the bulk of previous guidance. It has taken many years to get certain professional groups working together to protect children and it will be a slow task in the field of adult protection. This will not be helped by the lack of funding in adult protection work and the relative newness of the area to most agencies.

Intervention

As a result of *No Secrets*, many authorities are now giving staff training in investigating the abuse of vulnerable adults, although it is often shorter and less rigorous than the training given to child care workers. Until recently, there was a tendency for staff in adult services to emphasise the welfare side of abuse. Faced with an abusive situation, more support services would be arranged, and sometimes the confrontation of the abuser. Adult protection conferences and criminal action would be far from any plans. Homer and Gilleard (1990) have shown that this has not always been effective, and Brown et al. (1995) showed that out of 288 reported cases, there were only four convictions. Pritchard (1990) described a range of services that were offered in order to help victims rather than encouraging a legal response. The emphasis on avoiding disruption and confrontation, while motivated from a commitment to the perceived welfare of the vulnerable adult, has left some older people in unreasonable situations. It also has left the abuser free to move on and abuse elsewhere. Biggs (1996) stated that the use of care management as a response closes off other options. It leads to an emphasis on domestic abuse and solving the problem by dealing with carer stress through more support. The carer stress hypothesis is more comfortable for us and normalises abuse. Breckman and Adelman (1988) advocated a clear goal of an abuse-free life for the victim, and if necessary separation from the abuser to achieve this. However, the lack of an integrated view of intervention can go against this goal. There is a need for workers to see legal action and the provision of services as two of several viable options to safeguard the victim. Clough (1995) said that the two major principles should be maximum autonomy and minimum intervention.

This style of working sits uneasily alongside more joint working with the police. Social workers have not always felt confident in dealing with abuse in a manner which does not prejudice the future possible use of the criminal justice system. Decalmer and Glendenning (1997) advocate the use of a screening tool that includes leading questions which, if used, could prejudice the prospects of a criminal route to resolving the problem. When social workers deal with investigation without involving the police, forensic evidence can easily be lost and the possibility of criminal action adversely affected.

There is a similar gap in working with medical colleagues, and often investigations have not included the consideration of a full medical assessment. The specialist role of the paediatrician in child protection has no similar parallel in adult protection, and any knowledge and skills are spread thinly across specialisms. General practitioners largely remain ignorant of adult abuse. The lack of working with other agencies closely in adult protection is prevalent at every stage of the process. For example, in responding initially to a referral in child protection, inter-agency checks have long been seen as a fundamental part of the process but are greeted with surprise by many adult services staff and managers.

There has often been a lack of clarity about which stage of the response process staff are working within. This can lead to the wrong people acting without the appropriate skills. In the AIMS pack (2001) the distinct phases of referring, alerting and investigating are very useful in delineating the process. Many policies are now beginning to state that only suitably trained staff should work at investigation level.

The role of multi-agency conferences is not always clear in adult protection. Most policies include such a meeting, but these can range from low profile chats about clients, to conferences along the lines of child protection with rigorous procedures. Staff are often unclear about the difference between strategy meetings and conferences. Conferences tend only to be used in the more dramatic events such as physical and sexual abuse. It is even more useful to bring agencies together and form joint plans in the ongoing chronic situations of neglect and psychological abuse, but there is limited use in this area. Action on Elder Abuse (2006) demonstrated an under use of conferences. The value of a clear shared protection plan cannot be overemphasised. Pritchard (1996) said that protection plans must be developed, implemented and reviewed regularly. Pritchard (1999) quoted two vulnerable adults who said,

> *All hell broke loose. People came to talk to me for weeks on end. Then, nothing. I thought they were going to help me. Fat chance. Things are just as they were.*

It is important that the end goal of any intervention is to improve the situation of the vulnerable adult.

The use of adult protection registers is unusual in adult services. Child protection registers have long been an integral part of the intervention in child abuse, but the legal and human rights implications that adult protection registers have caused so far have stopped a similar development for adults.

Legal framework

The legal framework is significant despite the reluctance of many abused vulnerable adults to accept the legal alternative, due to fear or concern for the abuser's future. This has often led to legal remedies failing to be considered, which is very different from practice in domestic violence. There have been a number of recent changes in the law, with more planned for the future. *The Mental Health Act* 1983 is currently being reviewed, and could lead to important changes to some aspects of working with vulnerable adults. The present Act gives powers of access to approved social workers if the person is not *under proper care* (115), and offers protection to the mentally disordered from willful neglect or ill-treatment by carers (172), with a power of removal via a magistrate (135).

Who Decides (1997) had proposed radical changes with the introduction of emergency powers for incapacitated adults, but these were not taken forward in further guidance (*Making Decisions,* 1999). Many of the proposals were taken up in the Mental Capacity Act 2005 but emergency powers have only appeared again in a private members bill, Care of Older and Incapacitated Adults (human rights) Bill 2006, unlikely to come to fruition. This Bill and the current research findings may add to the pressure to make such changes.

The issue of mental capacity is critical in deciding action in adult protection. There is a presumption in English law that everyone has mental capacity until the contrary is proved. In undertaking investigations, capacity to consent is a key issue. There are two key capacity issues and the first is the capacity of the adult to consent to the sexual act or other act about which there is concern. If the adult has capacity and consented to the abusive act, it is unlikely that any prosecution can take place although the police should still be consulted. A vulnerable adult's capacity may fluctuate over time. This can be critical in determining whether an act is abusive or consenting. The second key area where capacity is significant is consent to the process of the investigation – active involvement of the police, interviews and medical assessment. If the vulnerable adult lacks capacity for this function, it is inappropriate for their consent to the process to be sought. However, they should be engaged with the process in any way possible. If the adult has capacity and declines assistance and refuses an investigation, actions will be limited. Such situations should be discussed at an Adult Protection Conference to ensure all agencies are aware of the risks and the danger signals.

In assessing capacity, it is important to distinguish between capacity to make the decision and the ability to communicate the decision. The Mental Capacity Act 2005 makes clear that a functional approach to capacity must be taken and the adult must be assessed in relation to their capacity for this specific decision, not a general assessment. The test is whether the person is capable of understanding the particular decision. If a particular decision is trivial, a low degree of understanding will suffice. The more complex the decision the greater understanding is needed.

The Mental Capacity Act has set five key principles which make it clear that a person should be seen as having capacity unless proven otherwise. These are as follows.

- A person must be assumed to have capacity unless it is established he lacks capacity.

- A person is not to be treated as unable to make decisions unless all practicable steps to help him to do so have been taken without success.

- A person is not to be treated as unable to make a decision merely because he makes an unwise decision.

- An act done, or decision made, under this Act for or on behalf of a person who lacks capacity must be done or made in his best interests.

- Before the act is done, or the decision made, regard must be had to whether the purpose for which it is needed can be as effectively achieved in a way that is less restrictive of the person's rights and freedom of action.

Someone is unable to make a decision for himself if he is unable

- to understand the information relevant to the decision

- to retain the information

- to use or weigh that information as part of the process of making the decision

- to communicate his decision by any means.

There is a best interests checklist for people acting on behalf of others. This includes the following.

- Consider whether it is likely that the person will at some time have capacity in relation to the matter in question and if so, when.

- They must permit and encourage the person to participate as fully as possible in any act and decision.

- They must consider the person's past and present wishes and feelings, the beliefs and values that would be likely to influence his decision if he had capacity and the other factors he would be likely to consider if he were able to do so.

- He must take account if it is practical and appropriate to consult them, the views of anyone named by the person for consultation, carers, donees of lasting power of attorney or court appointed deputies.

The Act has extended the Court of Protection's role to cover welfare matters, not just financial matters. After implementation in April 2007, a Lasting Power of Attorney will replace the Enduring Power of Attorney but can specify other decisions on wider welfare matters as well as finance. Most day to day informal decisions will be able to be taken without interference of the court, with a general authority resting on the carer. The Court can appoint deputies who would help with welfare and financial decisions where the person lost capacity without appointing a Lasting Power of Attorney. This replaces the current system of receivership covering financial decision-making and extends it to include health and welfare. The Act has created Independent Mental Capacity Advocates to support those lacking capacity who have no one else to speak for them when decisions are taken about serious medical treatment or long-term residential care. The Mental Capacity Act creates a new criminal offence of ill treatment or neglect of an adult who lacks mental capacity.

In general, *The Human Rights Act* 1998 has created some interesting challenges in the field of adult protection, leaving public authorities open to criticism either for failing to act to protect people from degrading or inhuman treatment or acting in a way which interferes with private and family life. Care in using correct procedures and gaining legal advice has resulted from this, and that has to be beneficial to vulnerable adults. *The Data Protection Act* 1998 has caused appropriate concern about the sharing of personal information, but it has to be remembered that information can still be shared where it is for the prevention or detection of a crime, even without the subject's consent. *The Crime and Disorder Act* 1998 Section 115 offers support to the practice of limited and responsible sharing of information in the joint agency process of detecting and preventing offences to victims. The Act means that disclosing information where this is necessary or expedient in preventing crime is still legal.

Other relevant general powers include *The National Health Service and Community Care Act* 1990 where Section 47 requires local authorities with Social Services Departments to carry out an assessment of need where people appear to be in need of community care services. *The Care Standards Act* 2000 has established a new, independent regulatory body for all social and health care services and will lead to a list of individuals unsuitable to work with vulnerable adults. For the first time, checks are now obligatory for those working with adults as well as children. The same act also will help with institutional abuse in terms of setting higher standards for care. T*he Disability Discrimination Act* 1996 makes it unlawful to discriminate against someone with a disability by treating them less favourably. It covers employment, training, education, housing and anyone who supplies goods, facilities and services to the public. There are also new provisions to protect whistle blowers from adverse effects on their employment in the *Public Interest Disclosure Act* (1998).

A useful legal option is the use of Declaratory Relief. This is where an authority needs a decision about some aspect of the care of an adult with mental incapacity and seeks a declaration from the Family Division of the High Court as to what is in the best interests of the adult. For example, Hackney sought *declaratory relief* when an 18 year old woman with learning disability and her mother were refusing Social Services help. There was evidence of harm, and the Court agreed it was lawful for her to be taken to residential care against the family's wishes. Just as pre-*Children Act* 1989, wardship orders were made when no other legislation provided the necessary powers; *declaratory relief* is now used to plug a gap in the existing law. This will probably become unnecessary with the implementation of the Mental Capacity Act and the increased use of the Court of Protection to make such welfare decisions.

Changes in adult protection law

The other big change in adult protection law in recent years has been the implementation of the *Sexual Offences Act* 2003 which repeals all previous legislation on sexual offences. Consent is a key issue in the Act and the freedom to make choices. The main sexual offences are rape (now including penile penetration of the mouth, anus or vagina), assault by penetration, sexual assault by touching and causing sexual activity without consent. Sexual relations with certain adult relatives have been clarified. There are a set of offences in relation to mentally disordered adults where choice is impeded. This includes adults with mental health problems or learning disability. There is specific protection from the misuse of a position of trust. It is an offence for someone who is in a relationship of care to have a sexual relationship with the mentally disordered adult.

In the area of neglect, there are limited powers. The use of the *National Assistance Act* 1948, section 47, has been used occasionally in relation to neglect or self-neglect. This allows the removal to suitable premises, people in need of care and attention who are:

> *suffering from chronic disease or, being aged, infirm or physically incapacitated and living in insanitary conditions and are unable to devote to themselves and are not receiving from other persons, proper care and attention.*

This has to be decided by the Community physician and is still an option even after the *Human Rights Act* 1998. *The Mental Health Act* 1983 makes it an offence to neglect or ill-treat those with mental disorder who are in hospital, nursing homes or subject to guardianship. *The Carers* (Recognition & Services) *Act* 1995 and all the provision for assessment and support of carers is of course relevant in reducing the risk of neglect in domestic situations.

In financial abuse, there are various criminal legislation provisions and other protective measures. Many offences constitute theft and need to be dealt with as such. *The Mental Capacity Act* also provides protection through Lasting Powers of Attorney and Deputies with far more safeguards built into these than previously.

In physical abuse, the *Family Law Act 1996* protects vulnerable and other adults in domestic violence situations. It provides for the making of Occupation Orders or non-molestation orders against anyone with whom the victim is 'associated' including spouses, cohabitees, co-tenants or relatives. The *Crime Victims and Domestic Violence Act* 2004 has added same sex relationships to this list and has also added a new criminal offence of causing or allowing the death of a vulnerable adult. There are many situations where domestic violence powers could be useful for vulnerable adults. All the criminal legislation in relation to assaults and violent crimes is relevant in working with physically abused vulnerable adults, and civil action can also be taken by an individual. Where a vulnerable adult is being threatened in some way the *Protection from Harassment Act* 1997 can be used to gain an order to help the victim.

Proposed changes

The limited emphasis on criminal routes to resolving adult abuse may alter in the future. *The Youth Justice and Criminal Evidence Act* 1999 and the consequent guidance issued by the Home Office (2001) mean that there is far more prospect of vulnerable adults being able to be heard in court. A series of special measures give many of the same provisions to vulnerable adults that children have had access to for some time. The use of video interviews as admissible evidence will be particularly beneficial for adults who have been abused, and will also make more demands for evidentially sound interviews. The provision in the Act does not of course only relate to abuse situations but to any witnessing of crimes. This therefore does not assume a role for a social worker. It is unclear yet how much joint working there will be between the police and social workers, with many areas developing separate training and guidance. As the police role in relation to vulnerable adults has been broadened and extended with the legislation, there is a danger that existing joint working practices are threatened.

Research into the use of special measures would suggest where they are used witnesses are more satisfied, but only 14% of uses are for those with illness or disability and 5% for adults with learning disability (Hamlyn et al. 2004). Burton et al. (2006) showed the police were finding it difficult to identify vulnerable and intimidated witnesses and there was limited use of video interviews. Special measures were often applied for very late which defeated the object of putting the mind of the vulnerable adult at ease.

Another alteration in the legal framework is proposed with greater checking of staff who are employed to work with vulnerable adults. The *Care Standards Act* introduced the Protection of Vulnerable Adults list which acts as a workforce ban. Staff who work in social care domiciliary or registered homes settings providing care can be referred to the list if they abuse, neglect or place adults at risk. The Commission for Social Care Inspection and the employer can refer workers to the list and they have the right of appeal. It is a criminal offence to apply to do any work with a vulnerable adult while on the list. This list was implemented in July 2004, but already there is dissatisfaction with the way unsuitable people are barred from working with children and vulnerable adults. *The Bichard Report* (2004) followed the murder of two children in Soham and has proposed some changes, now incorporated into the *Safeguarding Vulnerable Groups Bill* 2006. This is likely to create a new centralised vetting and barring scheme for those working with children or vulnerable adults. It will be a positive registration process and will be directly linked to current police information with an enhanced Criminal Records Bureau to check the point of entry.

Anti-oppressive practice

As in every area of social work, there is a need to reflect on anti-oppressive practice. Thompson's (1998) model shows the need to reflect broadly and look at both the macro and micro level analysis. For each specialist client group there will be different issues. For example, in looking at older people, it is evident that there is discrimination against this group at a structural level. There is the lack of medical prioritising of this group and the fact that it is considered common practice for age to be an accepted form of discrimination in employment. Recognising the structural factors in elder abuse avoids the historic tendency to focus on individual families and abusers. There is a need to acknowledge the factors in society which create dependency, particularly for older women. At the cultural level, jokes about older people and assumptions that all of them are confused and dependent are commonplace. At a personal level, despite the fact that we all hope one day to be older people, there is less awareness of discrimination and the need to counter it than for other groups. Discrimination has always been there for this group. Minois (1989) quotes a seventh century BC philosopher who said,

Happy are they who die at the age of 60 since once painful old age has arrived, which renders man ugly and useless, his heart is no longer free of evil cares.

Similarly, adults with learning disability have experienced a range of discrimination at all levels. Structurally, society disempowers this group with the law still not allowing certain choices to be made. Medical and financial decisions are often taken on behalf of people with learning disability, and culturally they are frequently treated in a child-like way. For example, parents are often still involved in decision-making in a way that many non-disabled adults would find unacceptable. *Valuing People,* issued by the Department of Health (2001), has promoted the need for real choices in relation to employment and housing, but this is a big jump culturally. At a personal level, prejudices can lead to adults with learning disability being assumed to be incompetent or disruptive.

For other vulnerable adult groups, oppressive notions in society lead to a lack of recognition of their vulnerability to abuse, as acknowledged in relation to those with mental health problems. Pritchard (2001) highlighted the lack of recognition given to male victims of abuse with all the attention going to women. Discrimination is not only out in the community. Social Services departments have often been guilty of emphasising and resourcing child protection in a way that is not seen in adult protection.

The need to empower service users while dealing with abuse can create appropriate and healthy tensions. Where adults have mental capacity they have choice, and this needs to be recognised without abdicating responsibility for linking with other agencies to promote protective practices. Pritchard (2001) reminds us of the need to ensure that referral of victims does not result in a *double whammy of abuse,* with an over-emphasis on self-determination justifying idleness by professional workers.

One of the factors to acknowledge within this discussion is the gender dimension of abuse. Old age affects men and women differently, with poverty and dependency a common theme for older women. The majority of older people are women and they tend to be poorer than men. Black women tend to be poorer, and to live in inner city areas with more social problems. Consequently women form the large majority of victims of elder abuse (Aitken and Griffin, 1996).

There is very little research on ethnic issues. McCreadie (2001) commented on the need for adult protection policies to highlight racial abuse and harassment, but few at the time of her studies did so. She also recommended there should be specific arrangements for responding to the abuse of ethnic minority elders. There is a lack of black older people in studies of adult abuse in British local authorities (SSI, 1992), which begs questions as to whether they are safer, or whether detection is more difficult. Many will be dealing with the effect of life-long racism on their self-esteem and will be more vulnerable to racist attacks in old age. Generally, age in the ethnic population is lower than in the white population, with black Caribbean the only substantial ethnic subdivision in older people. Ethnicity, age and gender issues are all interrelated with housing and family characteristics. There is not one single causative factor for adult abuse, but all these need to be considered.

Future and conclusion

There are many areas for further research, particularly in the sub-groups so far neglected, for example, those with mental health problems. There are also areas that need further development in policy terms, with clarification of the threshold for action. There is a need for specialist work to continue after an investigation takes place, with suitable support and, if necessary, therapy. This can be neglected in both child and adult protection. An area which has also had little attention thus far in adult protection is 'keeping safe work'. This is commonly undertaken with children to prevent abuse, by the raising of their levels of awareness and the development of protective skills. There has been a small amount of work of this kind for older people and those with learning disability, but this could be developed much further.

For the worker within the field of community care, it is important to keep adult abuse in the context of all other good work with vulnerable adults. Child protection has had to be balanced with an emphasis on refocusing services, and the need in adult protection is to place protective work within a framework of positive attention to the vulnerable adult's welfare. As policies and law develop to protect adults more effectively, it will be necessary to keep this balance. The current emphasis on adult protection is long overdue and needs to be firmly placed within a high standard of work with vulnerable adults to be of benefit to them.

References

Abberley, P. (1987) The concept of oppression and the development of a social theory of disability. *Disability, Handicap and Society*, Vol. 2 (187): 5–1.9.

Abercrombie, N. (2006) *Penguin dictionary of sociology*. Penguin: London.

Abrams, P. (1977) Community care. *Policy and politics*, 6.

Acheson, D. (1998) *Independent enquiry into inequalities in health*. London: HMSO.

Action on Elder Abuse (1995) *Everybody's business: taking action on elder abuse*. Action on Elder Abuse: London.

Action on Elder Abuse (2006) *Adult protection data collection and reporting requirements*. Action on Elder Abuse.

Adams, R. (2002) *Social policy for social work*. Palgrave.

Age Concern (2001) *Opening doors: older lesbian and gay people – forgotten no more*. London: Age Concern.

AIMS (2001) *Aims alerters' guide – complete guidance for staff involved in adult protection*. Pavilion.

Aitken, L. and Griffin, G. (1996) *Gender issues in elder abuse*. London: Sage Publications.

Allan, G. (1990) Social work, community care and informal networks, in Davies, M. (ed.) *The Sociology of Social Work*. London: Routledge.

Allan, G. (1985) *Family life*. Oxford: Basil Blackwell.

Alt, J.E. and Chrystal, K.A. (1983) *Political economics*. Brighton: Wheatsheaf.

American Association of Mental Retardation. (2002) *Definition of Mental Retardation* via www.aamr.org/Policies/mental_retardation.shtml accessed 10/03/2006.

American Psychiatric Association. (2000) *Diagnostic Static Manual IV Text Revised DSM IV-TR*. Washington DC: American Psychiatric Association.

Antrobus, D. (2001) *How can the circles of support model be adapted to fit into the existing Sheffield Direct Payments Scheme? www.vas.org.uk*

Arber, S. and Gilbert, M. (1989) *Men: the forgotten carers*. Sociology, 23, 1989.

Arevalo, M. (2001) Influences on health in J. Thompson and S. Pickering (eds.) *Meeting the health needs of people who have a learning disability*. London: Baillière Tindall.

Association of the Directors of Social Services (2005) *Safeguarding adults*.

Atherton, H. (2003) A history of learning disabilities, chapter 3 in B. Gates (ed.) (2003) *Learning disabilities* (4th ed). Edinburgh: Churchill Livingstone.

Atkin, K. (1991) Community care in a multi-racial society. *Policy and Politics*, 19, 3.

Audit Commission (1986) *Making a reality of Community Care*. London: Audit Commission.

Audit Commission (2002) Performance assessment section, front page.

Audit Commission (2004) Choice in public services, report.

Author unknown (2001) White Paper puts choice at heart of new learning difficulties strategy, *Community Care Magazine*, 2001, communitycare.co.uk.

Bailey, G., Erwin, L., Sanderson, H., Gorman, R. and Cobb, J. with the North West Person Centred Planning Coordinators Community of Practice. (2005) *Using person centred approaches to Health Action Plan*. www.valuingpeople.gov.uk/documents/ HAP&PCP.doc

Baker, A.A. (1975) *Granny battering, modern geriatrics,* 5(8): 20–4.

Baldock, J. and Ungerson, C. (1991) What d'ya want if ya'don't want money, in Mclean, M. and Groves, D. (eds.) *Women's Issues in Social Policy.* London: Routledge.

Baldock J. et al. (1990) *Care for the elderly: significant innovations in three European countries.* Boulder: Westview.

Baldwin, S. and Twigg, J. (1991) Women and community care – reflections on a debate, in Maclean, M. and Groves, D. (eds.) *Women's Issues in Social Policy*. London: Routledge.

Ball, A.R. and Peters, B.G. (2000) *Modern politics and government*, 6th ed. London: Macmillan.

Bank-Mikkelson, N. (1979) *The Danish mental retardation service. Paper 1: the quality of care. Report of a study tour*. London: National Society for Mentally Handicapped Children.

Banks, S. (1995) *Ethics and values in social work*. Hampshire: Macmillan Press.

Banks, S. (1995) in Skerrett, D. (2000 p63) Social work — a shifting paradigm. *Journal of Social Work Practice* Volume 14, No 1.

Barclay Report (1982) *The social basis of community care*. Winchester MA: Allen & Unwin.

Barclay Report (1982) *Social workers: their role and tasks.* London: Bedford Square Press.

Barnes, C., Mercer, G. and Shakespeare, T. (1999) *Exploring disability: a sociological Introduction.* Cambridge: Polity Press.

Barr, O., Gilgunn, J., Kane, T. and Moore, G., (1999). Health screening for people with learning disabilities by a community learning disability nursing service in Northern Ireland. *Journal of Advanced Nursing* 29: 1482–1491.

Barritt, A. (1990) *Innovations in community care*, London: FPSC.

Bartlett, W. et al. (eds.) (1994) *Quasi-markets in the welfare state*. Bristol: SAUS.

Barton, R. (1959) *Institutional neurosis*. Bristol: Wright.

Batty, D. (2002) Stars fail to illuminate, *Guardian*, 31 May.

Bayliss, K. (2000) Social work values, anti-discriminatory practice and working with older lesbian service users. *Social Work Education*, 19 (1): 45–53.

Beange, H. (1996). Caring for a vulnerable population: who will take responsibility for those getting a raw deal from the health care system? *Medical Journal of Australia*, 164: 159–160.

Beeler, J. A., Rawls, T.W., Herdt, G. and Cohler, B.J. (1999) The needs of older lesbians and gay men in Chicago. *Journal of Gay and Lesbian Social Services*. Vol. 9 (1): 31–49.

Bennett, G. and Kingston, P. (1993) *Elder abuse: concepts, theories and interventions*. London: Chapman and Hall.

Bennett, G., Kingston, P. and Penhale, B. (1997) *The dimensions of elder abuse*. London: Macmillan Press.

Beresford, P. and Branfield, F. (2004) Shape up and listen. *Community Care*, 4 Nov, : 40–41.

Berger, R.M. (1982) The unseen minority: older gays and lesbians. *Social Work*, Vol.27: 236–242.

Berkman, C.S. and Zinberg, G. (1997) Homophobia and heterosexism in social workers. *Social Work*, 42: 319–332.

Berlin, I. (1969) *Four essays on liberty*. Oxford: Oxford University Press.

Bevans, L. (2004) Social care supremo aims to put adult services back on the map. *Community Care*, 1 Jul: 16–17.

Beveridge, W. (1942) *The Beveridge Report*. London. HMSO.

Bewley, C. (1997) *Money matters – helping people with learning difficulties have more control over their money*. London: Values into Action.

The Bichard Inquiry Report (2004) London: The Stationery Office.

Biggs, S. (1993) User participation and interprofessional collaboration in community care. *Journal of Interprofessional*, Volume 7, No 2.

Biggs, S. (1996) A family concern: elder abuse in British social policy. *Critical Social Policy*, 16(2): 63–88.

Biggs, S., Phillipson, C. and Kingston, P. (1995) *Elder abuse in perspective*. Buckingham: Open University Press.

Binnie, A. and Titchen, A. (1999) *Freedom to practise: the development of patient centered nursing*. Butterworth Heinemann.

Blair, T. (1998) Third Way: new politics for a new century. *Fabian Pamphlet* 588. London: The Fabian Society.

Blair, T. (2004) Labour Party conference speech 11 October 2004.

Bohan, J. (1996) *Psychology and sexual orientation: coming to terms*. New York; London: Routledge.

Boxall, K. (2002) Individual and social models of disability and the experiences of people with learning difficulties, chapter 12 in D. RacE (ed.) (2002) *Learning disability: a social approach*. London: Routledge.

Bradshaw, J. (1972) The concept of social need. *New Society*, 30: 640–643.

Branford, D. (1994), A study of the prescribing for people with learning disabilities living in the community and in National Health Service care. *Journal of Intellectual Disability Research*, 38: 577–586.

Braye, S. and Preston-Shoot, M. (1995) *Empowering practice in social care.* Buckingham: Open University Press.

Brechin, A. (1981) *Handicap in a social world.* London: Hodder Arnold.

Brechin, A. (2000) *Critical practice in health and social care.* London: Sage.

Breckman, R. and Adelman, R. (1988) *Strategies for helping victims of elder mistreatment.* London: Sage Publications.

Brewster, J. and Ramcharan, P. (2005) Enabling and supporting person-centred approaches, chapter 24 in G. Grant, P. Gowar, M. Richardson and R. Ramcharan (eds.) (2005) *Learning disability: a lifestyle approach to valuing people.* Buckingham: OU Press.

Briere, J., Woo, R., McRae, B., Foltz, J. and Sitzman, R. (1997) Childhood sexual abuse and physical abuse as factors in adult psychiatric illness. *American Journal of Psychiatry, 144*: 1426–30.

Briggs, S. (1991) Community care, case management and the psychodynamic perspective. *Journal of Social Work Practice*, 5(1): 71–81.

Brotman, S., Ryan, B. and Cormier, R. (2003) The health and social service needs of gay and lesbian elders and their families in Canada. *The Gerontologist*, 43 (2): 192–202.

Brown, H., Kingston, P. and Wilson, B. (1999) Adult protection: an overview of research and policy. *The Journal of Adult Protection*, 1(1).

Brown, H. and Stein, J. (1998) Implementing adult protection policies in Kent and East Sussex. *Journal of Social Policy,* 27(3): 371–96.

Brown, H., Stein, J. and Turk, V. (1995) The sexual abuse of adults with learning disabilities: report of a second two year incidence survey. *Mental Handicap Research*, **8**(1): 3–24.

Brown, H. and Turk, V. (1992) Defining sexual abuse as it affects adults with learning disabilities. *Mental Handicap,* 20; 44–55.

Brown, H. and Turk, V. (1993) *It could never happen here: the prevention and treatment of sexual abuse of adults with learning disabilities in residential settings.* Chesterfield: Association for Residential Care and National Association for the Protection from Sexual Abuse of Adults and Children with Learning Disabilities.

Bulmer, M. (1986) *Neighbours: the work of Phillip Abrams.* Cambridge University Press.

Bulmer M. (1987) *The social basis of community care.* Winchester MA: Allen & Unwin.

Burke, B. and Harrison, P. (2002) Anti-oppressive practice, in R. Adams, L. Dominelli and M. Payne (eds.) *Social work: themes, issues and critical debates* (2nd ed) London: Palgrave.

Burnham, D. (2004) On target? *Community Care*, 26 Feb: 34–35.

Burton, Evans and Sanders (2006) *Evaluation of the use of special measures.* Home Office.

Butler, J. (1994) Origins and early development, in Robinson, R. and Le Grand, J. (eds.) *Evaluating the NHS reforms*. Newbury: King's Fund Institute.

Cabinet Office (2005) I*mproving the life chances of disabled people. A joint report of Department of Health, Department of Work and Pensions, and the Office of the Deputy Prime Minister* www.strategy.gov.uk/downloads/work_areas/disability/disability_report/pdf/disability.pdf

Camden and Islington Community Health Services NHS Trust (1999) *Beech House inquiry report of the internal inquiry relating to the mistreatment of patients residing at Beech House, St Pancras Hospital during the period March 1993 – April 1996.* London: Camden and Islington Community Health Services NHS Trust.

Carter, G. and Jancar, J. (1983) Mortality in the mentally handicapped: a 50 year survey at the Stoke Park group of hospitals (1930–1980). *Journal of Mental Deficiency Research*, 27: 143–156.

Carvel, J. (2005) Steps in the right direction, *Guardian*. 30 Nov online. Available at *www.society.guardian.co.uk/socialcare/story/07890,1653428* (accessed 01–12–05).

Casement, P. (1985) in Bray, S. and Preston-Shoot, M. (1995) *Empowering practice in social care*. Open University Press.

CCETSW (1989) *Multi disciplinary teamwork, models of good practice.*

CCETSW (1996) *Equal opportunities policy statement.*

Chaplin, R.H., Thorp, C., Ismail, I.A., Collacott, R.A. and Bhaumik, S. (1996) Psychiatric disorder in Asian adults with learning disabilities: patterns of service use. *Journal of Intellectual Disability Research*, 40: 298–304.

Chapman, T. et al. (1991) *A new deal for the mentally Ill?.* JSP, Aug.

Clarke, D.J., Kelly, S., Thinn, K. and Corbett, J.A. (1990) Psychotropic drugs and mental retardation. *Journal of Mental Deficiency Research*, 34: 385–395.

Clarke, H. and Spafford, J. (2002) Adapting to the culture of user control? *Social Work Education*, 2002, Volume 21, No.2, 247–257, Carfax Publishing.

Clarke, J. (1998) Thriving on chaos, in Carter, J. (ed.) *Post-modernity and the Fragmentation of Welfare*. New York: Routledge.

Clarke, J. and Newman, J. (1998) *The managerial state*. London: Sage Publications.

Clarke J. Gerwitz,S. and McLaughlin, E. (eds.) (2000) *New managerialism, new welfare?* London: Sage Publications (in association with the Open University.)

Clifford, D. (1991) *The social costs and rewards of caring*. Aldershot: Brookfield.

Clough R. (1995) Forward – elder abuse and the law. Paper presented at the First Annual Conference of Action on Elder Abuse, Lancaster University 1994. *Community Care,* 16 May 2000.

Cochrane, A. (1998) Globalisation, fragmentation and local welfare citizenship, in Carter, J. (ed.) *Post-modernity and the fragmentation of the welfare state*. New York: Routledge.

Cole, T. (1999) *Wealth, poverty and welfare*. London: Hodder and Stoughton.

Commission for Social Care Inspection (2004) *Direct Payments. What are the Barriers?*, www.csci.org.uk

Community Care (2003) New ratings reveal rise in standards. *Community Care*, 13 Nov: 6.

Community Care (2004a) Pay benchmarks for workforce urged. *Community Care*, 4 Nov: 14.

Community Care (2004b) Ladyman tipped to publish adult services green paper by end of year. *Community Care*, 4 Nov: 14.

Community Care (2004c) Councils unhappy at area agreement rush. *Community Care*, 2 Dec: 12.

Conroy, J.W. and Adler, M. (1998) Mortality among Pennhurst class members, 1978–1989. *Mental Retardation*, 36: 380–385.

Cook-Daniels, L. (1997) Lesbian, gay male, bisexual and transgendered elders: elder abuse and neglect issues. *Journal of Elder Abuse and Neglect*, Vol.9 (2): 35–49.

Corbett, J. (1989) The quality of life in the independence curriculum disability, in what's so great about independence? French, S. (1991) *The New Beacon* Vol 75, no 886: 153–6.

Cornes, M. and Clough, R. (2004) Inside multi-disciplinary practice: challenges for single assessment. *Journal of Integrated Care*, 12, 2: 3–13.

Cowen, H. (199) *Community care, ideology and social policy*. London: Prentice Hall.

Creswell, S. (1996) *Community Care* 2 May 1996.

Crosland, C.A.R. (1956) *The future of Socialism.* London: Jonathan Cape.

Crosland, C.A.R.(1974) *Socialism now and other essays*. London: Jonathan Cape.

Crossman, R. (1977) *Crossman: the diaries of a cabinet minister vol. III 1968–1970*. London: Hamish Hamilton.

Cumming, E. and Henry, W. (1961) *Growing old: the process of disengagement*. New York: Basic Books.

Curnock, K. and Hardiker, P. (1979) *Towards practice theory: skills and methods in social assessments*. London: Routledge.

Dale, N. (1996) *Working with families, children with special needs*. Routledge.

Dalley, G. (1988) *Ideologies of caring*. Basingstoke: Macmillan Education.

Dalrymple, J. and Burke, B. (1996) *Anti-oppressive practice. Social care and the law.* Open University Press.

Daly, M and Lewis, J. (1998) Conceptualising social care and welfare state restructuring, in Lewis, J. (ed) (1998) *Gender, Social care and welfare state restructuring in Europe*. Aldershot: Ashgate.

Daly, M. and Lewis, J. (2000) The concept of social clue and the analysis of welfare states. *British Journal of Sociology*, 51(2): 281–298.

D'Augelli, A.R., Grossman, A.H., Hershberger, S. and O'Connell, T.S. (2001) Aspects of mental health among older lesbian, gay and bisexual adults. *Aging and Mental Health*, 5 (2):149–158 .

David, M. (1986) in Levitas R., *The New Right*. Cambridge: Polity Press.

Davies, M. (ed) (1991) *The sociology of social work.* London: Routledge.

Davies, C. et al. (1999) *Challenging practice in Health and Social care*. Sage Publications.

Davies, D. (1996) Homophobia and heterosexism, in Davies, D. and Neal, C. (ed.) *Pink Therapy: a guide for counsellors and therapists working with lesbian, gay and bisexual clients.* Buckingham: Open University Press.

Davies, N. and Duff, M. (2001) Breast cancer screening in intellectual disability. *Journal of Intellectual Disability Research,* 45: 253–257.

Deacon, J. (1974) *Tongue tied. Fifty years of friendship in a subnormality hospital.* London: National Society for Mentally Handicapped Children.

Deacon, S., Minichiello, V. and Plummer, D. (1995) Sexuality and older people: revisiting the assumptions. *Educational Gerontology,* Vol.21: 497–513.

Dean, H. (1996) *Welfare, Law and Citizenship*. Hertfordshire: Harvester Wheatsheaf.

Decalmer, P. and Glendenning, F. (1997) *The mistreatment of elderly people*. London: Sage Publications.

Department of Health (1987) *Promoting better health.* London: HMSO.

Department of Health. (1989) *Caring for people: Community care in the next decade and beyond*. Cmm 849. London: Department of Health.

Department of Health (1990) *The NHS and Community Care Act*. London: HMSO.

Department of Health (1993) *No longer afraid, the safeguard of elderly people in domestic settings*: practice guidelines. London: HMSO.

Department of Health (1996) *The 1996 Community Care (Direct Payments) Act*. London: HMSO.

Department of Health (1998) *Modernising social services: promoting independence, improving protection, raising standards.* CM 4169, London: Stationery Office.

Department of Health (1998) Modernising social services, executive summary.

Department of Health (1998) Moving into the Mainstream. London: Department of Health.

Department of Health (1998) *Signposts for Success*. London: Department of Health.

Department of Health (1999) *Caring about carers – a national strategy for carers*. London: Department of Health.

Department of Health (1999) The NHS plan TSO. London.

Department of Health (1999a) *Once a day*. London: Department of Health.

Department of Health (1999b) *Independent inquiry into inequalities in health report*. The London: Stationery Office.

Department of Health (1999) *Working together to safeguard children, a guide to inter-agency working to safeguard and promote the welfare of children*. London: HMSO.

Department of Health (2000) *No secrets: guidance on developing and implementing multi-agency policies and procedures to protect vulnerable adults from abuse*. London: HMSO.

Department of Health (2001) *National services framework for older people*. London: Department of Health.

Department of Health (2001) *The single assessment process guidance for local implementation: consultation draft*. London: HMSO.

Department of Health (2001) *Valuing people, a new strategy for learning disability for the 21st century*. London: HMSO.

Department of Health (2001a) *Valuing people: improving life chances for people with learning disabilities for the 21st century:* CMM 5086. London: Department of Health.

Department of Health (2001b) *Essence of care: patient focused bench-marking for health care*. Department of Health. London.

Department of Health (2002). *Action for health – health action plans and health facilitation. Detailed good practice guidance on implementation for learning disability partnership boards*. The Stationary Office: London.

Department of Health (2002) *Fair access to care services: policy guidance*. London: Department of Health.

Department of Health (2002) *Guidance on the single assessment process for older people*, HSC2002/001:LAC (2002). London: Department of Health.

Department of Health (2002) *Personal social services performance indicators*.

Department of Health (2003) *Direct Payments guidance: community care, services for carers and children's services (Direct Payments) guidance England*. London: Department of Health Publications.

Department of Health (2003) *The community care (delayed discharge etc) Act 2003: guidance for implementation*, HSC2003/009:LAC(2003)21. London: Department of Health.

Department of Health (2004) *Direct choices: what councils need to make direct payments happen for people with learning disabilities*. London: Department of Health Publications.

Department of Health (2004a) *Valuing people: moving forward together*. London: Department of Health.

Department of Health (2004b) *Choosing health: making healthy choices easier*. London: Department of Health.

Department of Health (2005) *Independence, well-being and choice: our vision for the future of social care for adults in England*. Cm 6499. London: HMSO.

Department of Health (2005) *Mental Incapacity Act*. London: Department of Health.

Department of Health (2005b) Press release 25 Nov 2005 – new tsar with learning disabilities to be appointed. www.dh.gov.uk/PublicationsAndStatistics/PressReleases/Press ReleasesNotices/fs/en?CONTENT_ID= 4123793&chk=EU3SHW

Department of Health (2005c) *Valuing people: making things better. The government's annual report on learning disability 2005.* www.dh.gov.uk/assetRoot/04/12/38/ 69/04123869.pdf

Department of Health (2005a) Valuing people support team: *Key highlights of research evidence on the health of people with learning disabilities.*www.valuingpeople. gov.uk/ documents/HealthKeyHighlights.doc

Department of Health (2006) Your health, your care, your say research report Jan 2006. www.dh.gov.uk/assetRoot/04/12/74/62/04127462.pdf

Department of Health and Social Security (1971) *Better services for the mentally handicapped.* Cmm 4683. London: HMSO.

Department of Social Security (1998) *A New Contract for Welfare.* CM 3805. London: Stationery Office.

DHSS (1981) *Report Growing Older.* London: HMSO.

DHSS (1984) *The enabling role of Social Service deptartments.* London: HMSO.

DHSS (1986) Cumberledge Report *Neighbourhood Nursing.* London: HMSO.

DHSS (1989) White Paper: *Caring for People.* London: HMSO.

Dill, A. (1993) Defining needs, defining systems: a critical analysis. *The Gerontologist,* 33(4):453–60.

Disability Discrimination Act. (1995) via Office of Public Sector information www.opsi.gov.uk/acts/acts1995/1995050.htm

Disability Rights Commission (2005) Changing Britain for good, putting disability at the heart of public policy. www.drc.org.uk/disabilitydebate/uploads/Changing_Britain_ for_Good_GB.pdf

Djuretic, T., Laing-Moton, T., Guy, M. And Gill M. (1999) Concerted effort is needed to ensure these women use preventive services. *British Medical Journal,* 318: 536.

Dominelli, L. (1993) *Social work: mirror of society or its conscience?* Sheffield: Department of Sociological Studies.

Doody, G.A., Johnstone, E.C., Sanderson, T.L., Cunningham-Owens, D.G. And Muir, W.J. (1998). 'Pfropfschizophrenie' revisited: schizophrenia in people with mild learning disability. *British Journal of Psychiatry,* 173: 145–153.

Doucette, J. (1986) *Violent acts against disabled women.* Toronto, Ontario: Disabled Women's Network (DAWN).

Dow, J. (2004) Direct Payments, *Journal of Integrated Care,* 2004, Volume 12, Issue 2. 20–23. Brighton: Pavilion Publishing.

Driver, S. and Martell, L. (1998) *New Labour. Politics after Thatcherism.* London: Polity Press.

Dunn (1985) in Thompson, N (2000 p17) *Theory and practice: thinking and doing in human services*. Buckingham: Open University Press.

Dyslexia Institute (2005) *The incidence of hidden disabilities in the prison population: Yorkshire and Humberside research* www.dyslexia-inst.org.uk/pdffiles/Hidden%20 Disabilities%20Prison.pdf

Eastman, M. (1984) *Old age abuse*. Mitcham: Age Concern.

Edgerton, R. (1975), Issues relating to the quality of life among mentally retarded persons in M. Begab and S. Richardson (eds) (1975) *The mentally retarded person in society: a social science perspective*. Baltimore: University Park Press.

Ellison, N. and Pierson, C. (eds) (1998) *Developments in British social policy*. London: Macmillan.

Emerson, E. (2001) *Challenging behaviour: analysis and intervention in people with severe intellectual disabilities* (2nd edn.). Cambridge: Cambridge University Press.

Emerson E., Malam B., Davies I. and Spencer K. (2005) *A survey of adults with a learning disability in 2003–4*. National Statistics and NHS Health and Social Care Information accessed via DOH at www.dh.gov.uk/PublicationsAndStatistics/Published Survey/ListOfSurveySince1990/GeneralSurveys/GeneralSurveysArticle/fs/en?CONTENT_ID = 4081207&chk=u%2Bd5fv

Equal Opportunities Commission (1982) *Caring for the elderly and handicapped*. Manchester: EOC.

Esping-Anderson, G. (1990) *The three worlds of welfare capitalism.* Cambridge: Polity Press.

Evandrou, M. (1990) *Challenging the invisibility of carers*. London: LSE.

Faculty of Public Health Medicine (2001) *Good public health practice*. Available at: www.fphm.org.uk/prof_standards/downloads/general_standards/C_Standards_for_ Organisations.pdf

Falvey, M.A., Forest, M., Pearpoint, J. and Rosenberg, R.L. (1997) *All my life's a circle: using the tools: circles, maps and path*. Toronto: Inclusion Press.

Featherstone, M. and Wernick, A. (1995) *Images of aging: cultural representations of later life*. London: Routledge.

Fenge, L. (2001) Empowerment and Community Care – projecting the 'voice' of older people. *Journal of Social and Family Welfare Law*, 23,4: 427–439.

Fennell, G. et al. (1988) in Thompson, N. (1993 p17) *Anti-discriminatory practice*. Macmillan.

Financial Times (2004) *Brown's pledge on welfare state*. Financial Times, 3; Dec: 1

Finch, A. (1984) *Community care: developing non-sexist alternatives*. CSP, 9.

Finch, J. (1989) *Family obligation and social change*. London: Polity Press.

Finch, J and Groves, D. (1980) *Community care and the family.* JSP, 9, 4: 494.

Finkelhor, D. and Pillemer, K.A. (1988) Elder abuse: its relationship to other forms of domestic violence, in Hotaling, G.T., Finkelhor, D., Kirkpatrick, J.T. and Straus, M.A.

(eds.), *Family abuse and its consequences: new directions in research*. London: Sage Publications.

Finkelstein, V. (1990) "We are not disabled, you are !", in S. Gregory and S. Hartley (eds.) (1990) *Constructing Deafness*. London: Pinter.

Finkelstein, V. and French, S. (1993) Towards a psychology of disability, in J. Swain. V. Finkelstein, S. French and M. Oliver (eds.) (1993) *Disabling Barriers, Enabling Environments*. London: Sage.

Finlayson, G. (1994) *Citizen, state and social welfare in Britain 1830–1990*. Oxford: Clarendon Press.

Finnister, G. (1991) Care in the community: the social security issues. *Social Work and Social Welfare*. Y1 B113.

Fisher, K. (2004) Health disparities and mental retardation. *Journal of Nursing Scholarship*. First Quarter: 48–53.

Flynn, N. (1989) The New Right and social policy, *Policy and Politics*, 17 (2): 97–109.

Foster, P. (1991) Resident care for frail elderly people: a positive reassessment. *Social Policy and Administration*, 251:2.

Foundation for people with learning disabilities (2004) *Fundamental facts: all the latest facts and figures on learning disabilities.* Foundation for People with Learning Disabilities, 2004 www.learningdisabilities.org.uk/page.cfm?pagecode=ISBISTMT

Freire, P. (1972) *Pedagogy of the oppressed*. Harmondsworth: Penguin.

Fulcher, J. (1999) British capitalism in the 1980s. Old times or new times?. *British Journal of Sociology,* 46 (2): 325–338.

Fullmer, E., Shenk, D. and Eastland, L. (1999) Negating identity: a feminist analysis of the social invisibility of older lesbians. *Journal of Women and Aging*, Vol. 11, 2–3: 131–148.

Galton F. (1883) Inquiries into human faculty and its development in B. Gates (ed.) (2003) *Learning disabilities* (4th ed.), Edinburgh: Churchill Livingstone.

Gates, B. (ed) (2003) *Learning disabilities* (4th ed). Edinburgh: Churchill Livingstone.

Geelen, R. and Soons, P. (1996) Rehabilitation and 'everyday' motivation model in *Patient education and counselling* (1996) p69–77.

Gelb, S. (1995) The beast in man; degeneration and mental retardation 1900–1920. *Mental Retardation* 33(1): 1–9.

George, V. and Wilding, P. (1985) *Ideology and social welfare*, 2d ed. Boston: RKP.

George, V. and Wilding, P. (1994) *Welfare and ideology.* Hertfordshire: Harvester Wheatsheaf.

Gibbs, J., Evans, M. and Rodway, S. (1987) *Report of the inquiry into Nye Bevan Lodge.* London: Borough of Southwark.

Giddens, A. (2000) Antony Giddens and Will Hutton in conversation, in Hutton, W. and Giddens, A. (eds.) (2000) *On the edge. Living with global capitalism*. London: Jonathan Cape.

Gilbert N. (1983) *Capitalism and the welfare state*. New Haven: Yale.

Gilbert, T. (1993) Learning disability nursing: from normalization to materialism – towards a new paradigm. *Journal of Advanced Nursing* (18): 1604–1609.

Glasby, J. (2004) Social services and the single assessment process: early warning signs? *Journal of Interprofessional Care*, 18,2: 129–39.

Glasby, J. and Littlechild, R. (2002) *Social work and Direct Payments.* Bristol: The Policy Press.

Glendinning C. (1990) Dependency and interdependency, the incomes of informal carers and the impact of Social Security. *JSP*, 19:4.

Glendinning, C. and Baldwin, S. (1988) in Walker, R. and Parker, G. (eds.) *Money Matters*. London: Sage.

Glendinning, C., Halliwell, S., Jacobs, S., Rummery, K. and Tyrer, J. (2000) New kinds of care, new kinds of relationships, how purchasing services affects relationships in giving and receiving personal assistance, in *Health and Social Care in the Community,* 2000, Volume 8(3), 201–211. Blackwell Science.

Glennerster, H. et al. (1994) GP fund holding: wild card or winning hand? in Robinson, R. and Le Grand, J. (eds) *Evaluating the NHS reforms.* Newbury: King's Fund Institute.

Glennesterm, H. et al. (1990) How much do we care? *Social Policy and Administration* 24: 2.

Goffman, E. (1961) *Asylums*. Harmondsworth: Penguin.

Goodwin, S. (1989/1990) Community Care..., *Journal of Social Policy*, 18, 1.

Gorman, H. (2000) Winning hearts and minds?- Emotional labour and learning for care management work. *Journal of Social Work Practice*, 14,2: 149–158.

Gramlich, S., McBride, G., Snelham, N. and Myers, B. (2002) *Journey to independence. What self advocates tell us about Direct Payments.* Worcestershire: BILD Publications.

Granada TV *Silent Minority* – TV Documentary. Broadcast ITV 1980.

Green, N. (1996) in Secker, J. et al. (2003 p382) Promoting independence: but promoting what and how? *Ageing and Society* 23, 2003: 375–391. Cambridge University Press.

Griffiths Report (1998) *Community care: agenda for action*. London: HMSO.

Haddon, M. (2004) The curious incident of the dog in the night-time. New York: Vintage USA. *Journal of professionalism and elderly people, Ageing and Society*, 14 (2): 237–53.

Hadley, R. and Hatch, S. (1981) *Social welfare and the failure of the state*. London: George & Unwin.

Hamlyn, Phelps and Sattar (2004) *Survey of vulnerable and intimidated witnesses.* Home Office.

Hard, S. and Plumb, W. (1987) Sexual abuse of persons with developmental disabilities, quoted in Turk, V. and Brown H. (1993) The sexual abuse of adults with learning disabilities: results of a two year incidence survey. *Mental Handicap Research*, 6: 193–216.

Harlow, E. (2003) New managerialism, Social Services departments and social work pratice today. *Practice*, 15(2): 29–44.

Harris, J. (1998) *Managing state social work: front-line management and the Labour process perspective*. Ashgate.

Harris, J. and Mcdonald, C. (2000) Post-Fordism, the Welfare State and the personal social services: a comparison of Australia and Britain, in *British Journal of Social Work*, 30(1), 51–70.

Harrison, S. and Pollitt, C. (1994) *Controlling health professionals*. Buckingham: Open University Press.

Hasler, F. (2003) *Clarifying the evidence on Direct payments into practice*. www.ncil.org.uk

Hasler, F., Campbell, J. and Zarb, G. (1999) *Direct routes to independence. A guide to local authority implementation and management of Direct Payments.* London: Policy Studies Institute.

Hassiotis, A., Barron, P. and O'Hara, J. (2000) Mental health services for people with learning disabilities: a complete overhaul is needed with strong links to mainstream services. *British Medical Journal*, 321: 583–584.

Hayden, M.F. (1998) Mortality among people with mental retardation living in the United States: research overview and policy application. *Mental Retardation,* 26: 345–359.

Hayek, F.A. (1960) *The constitution of liberty*. Chicago: University of Chicago Press.

Hayes, D. (2004) Numbers game straining relations between health and social services. *Community care*, Feb: 18–19.

Hays, T., Fortunato, V. and Minichiello, V. (1997) Insights into the lives of older gay men: a qualitative study with implications for practitioners. *Venereology*, Vol. 10, No.2: 115–120.

Healy, K. (2002) Managing human services in a market environment: what role for Social Workers?. *British Journal of Social Work*, 32(5).

Heaphy, B., Yip, A. and Thompson, D. (2003) *Lesbian, gay and bisexual lives over 50.* Nottingham Trent University: York House Publications.

Heng, S. (2004) The Simon Heng column. *Community Care*, 2 Dec: 22–23

Herring, R. and Thom, B. (1997) The right to take risks: alcohol and older people. *Social Policy and Administration*, 31(3): 233–46.

Hill, M. (1991) (ed.) *Social work and the European community.* London: Jessica Kingsley Publishers.

Hills, J. (1997) *The future of welfare*. York: Joseph Rowntree Foundation.

Hindess, B. (1987) *Freedom, equality and the market*. London: Tavistock Publications.

HM Treasury (2004) Releasing resources to the front/me, Independent review of public sector efficiency.

Holland, S. (1980) *The Socialist challenge. London*: Quartet Books.

Hollins, S., Attard, M.T., von Fraunhofer, N., McGuigan S. and Sedgwick (1998) Mortality in people with learning disabilities: risks, causes and death certification findings in London, in R. Northway, C, Hutchinson, A. Kingdon (2005) *A vision for learning disability nurses. A discussion document.* The United Kingdom learning disability consultant nurse network.

Holman, A. (1999) Direct Payments: the power to empower. *Llais (Autumn)*:3–6.

Holman, B. (2004) If only the radicals had stayed that way. *Community Care*, 30 Sept: 34–35.

Home Office (2000) *Setting the boundaries*. London: Home Office Communication Directorate.

Home Office (2001) *Achieving best evidence in criminal proceedings: guidance for vulnerable or intimidated witnesses including children*. London: Home Office Communication Directorate.

Homer, A.C. and Gilleard, C. (1990) Abuse of elderly people by their carers. *British Medical Journal*, **301**: 1359–62.

Hopson, B. (1981) in Herbert, M. (1986 p154) *Psychology for Social Workers.*

Howard, M. (2004) Interview, *Newsnight*, BBC 2, 22 Nov. 23:05hrs.

Howe, D. (1994) Modernity, post-modernity and social work. *British Journal of Social Work*, 24: 513–532.

Howells, G. (1996) Situations vacant: doctors required to provide care for people with learning disability. *British Journal of General Practice*, 46, 403: 59–60.

Hudson, B. (1989) *The Health Service Journal*, 14/28: 1546.

Hudson, B. (1991) A question of teamwork. *Health Service Journal*, 4 April.

Hudson, W and Ricketts, W. (1980) A strategy for the measurement of homophobia, *Journal of Homosexuality*, 5: 357–372.

Hughes, G. (1998) A suitable case for treatments? Constructions of disability in E. Saraga (1998) (ed.) *Embodying the social: constructions of difference*. London: Routledge.

Hugman, R. (1994) Social work and case management in the UK: models of professionalism and elderly people. *Ageing and Society*, 14(2) 237–53.

Human Rights Act (1998) Office of Public Sector Information. www.opsi.gov.uk/acts/acts1998/19980042.htm

Hunter, M. (2001) Single assessment process: will Social Services suffer in new regime? *Community Care*, 23–29 August: 10–11.

Hutton, W. (1995) *The state we're in*. London: Vintage.

Hutton, W. and Giddens, A. (eds.) (2000) *On the edge. Living with global capitialism*. London: Jonathan Cape.

Jack, R. (1994) Dependence, power and violation: gender issues in abuse of elderly people by formal carers, in M. Eastman (ed) *Old age abuse: a new perspective*. London: Chapman Hall.

Jack, R. (1998) Institutions in community care, in Jack, R. (ed) *Residential v. community care*. Basingstoke: MacMillan.

Jacobs, R. J., Rasmussen, L. A. and Hohman, M. (1999) The social support needs of older lesbians, gay men, and bisexuals. *Journal of Gay and Lesbian Social Services*. Vol. (1): 1–30.

Jamieson, A. and Illsley, R. (1990) *Contrasting European policies for the care of older people*. Aldershot: Avebury Gower Publishing.

Jay, P. (1979) *Report of the committee of enquiry into mental handicap nursing and care*. Cmnd 7468. London: Department of Health and Social Security.

Johnson, M. (1990) The mixed economy of welfare, in Ware, A. and Goodin, R.E. *Needs and Welfare* (1990) London: Sage.

Johnson, N. (1990) *Reconstructing the welfare state*. Hertfordshire: Simon and Shuster.

Johnson, N. (1995) Domestic violence: an overview, in Kingston, P. and Penhale, B. (eds) *Family violence and the Caring Professions*. Basingstoke: Macmillan.

Jones, C. (2002) Social work and society, in Adams, R., Dominelli, L. and Payne, M. (eds.) (2002) *Social work: themes, issues and critical debates 3rd ed*. London: Palgrave.

Jones, K. (1989) *Experience in mental health*. London: Sage.

Jones, K. (1998) We need the bed – continuing care and community care, in Jack, R. (ed) *Residential v. community care*. Basingstoke: MacMillan.

Jones, S. (1999) Learning disability nursing – holistic care at its best. *Nursing Standard,* 13 (52): 61–63.

Jordan, B. (1998) *The new politics of welfare*. London: Sage Publications.

Jordan, B. (2000) *Social work and the Third Way: tough love as social policy*. Sage Publications.

Jordan, B. (2004) Emancipatory social work? Opportunity or oxymoron. *British Journal of Social Work*, 34: 5–19.

Jordan, B. and Jordan, C. (2000) *Social work and the Third Way*. Tough love as social policy. London: Sage.

Jordan, U. (2001) Tough love: social work, social exclusion and the Third Way, *British Journal of Social Work*, 2001, Volume 31, 527–546, Oxford University Press.

Joseph Rowntree Foundation (1999) *Implementing Direct Payments for People with Learning Difficulties*. Findings, 1999, www.jrf.org.uk

Kappeler (1995) *The will to violence: the politics of personal behaviour*. Cambridge: Polity Press.

Kelly, J. (1977) The aging male homosexual: myth and reality. *The Gerontologist*, Vol. 17: 328–332.

Kemshall, H. (1984) *Defining clients' needs in social work*. Social Work Monographs, Norwich: University of East Anglia.

Kemshall, H. (2002) *Risk, social policy and welfare*. Buckingham: Open University Press.

Kemshall, H. and Pritchard, J. (eds.) (1996) *Good practice in risk assessment and risk management*. London: Jessica Kingsley Publishers.

Kenny, C. (2004) Councils pushing patients through hospitals' revolving doors. *Community Care*, 28 Oct: 18–19.

Keynes, J. M. (1936) *The general theory of employment, interest and money*, London: Macmillan.

Killin, D. (1993) Independent living, personal assistance, disabled lesbians and gay men, in C. Barnes (ed.) *Making our own choices: independent living, personal assistance and disabled people*. Belper: BCODP.

Kings Fund, The (2002) Rehabilitation and intermediate care: policy documents. London.

Kirby, J. (2000) in Wade, S. and Lees, L. (2002, p7) The who, why, what of intermediate care. *Journal of Community Nursing*, October 2002 Volume 16; issue 10.

Kumar, S. (2004) Fear for care packages as staff feel the pressure of discharge targets. *Community Care*, 17 Jun: 10.

Kushlik, A. (1970) Residential care for the mentally subnormal. *Royal Society of Health Journal* (90): 223–34.

Kuttner, R. (2000) *The role of governments in the global economy*, in Hutton and Giddens, (eds.) (2000).

Ladyman, S. (2004) Vision validated (p44) *Community Care*, 7–13 October 2004.

Land, H. (1989) in Bulmer, M. *The goals of social policy*. London: Unwin.

Langan, M. (1990) Community care in the 1990s. *Critical Social Policy*, 29.

Langen M. (1998) (ed.) *Welfare: needs, rights and risks*. London: Routledge.

Langley, J. (1997) *Meeting the needs of older lesbians and gay men*. University of Brighton: Health and Social Policy Research Centre.

Langley, J. (2001) Developing anti-oppressive practice empowering social work practice with older lesbian women and gay men. *British Journal of Social Work*, 31: 917–932.

Lau, E. and Kosberg, J.I. (1979) Abuse of the elderly by informal care providers. *Ageing*, September/October: 11–15.

Laverack, G. (2004) *Health promotion practice: power and empowerment*. London: Sage Publications.

Leaper, R. (1971) *Community work*. National Council of Social Services.

Learning Disability Taskforce (2004) *Rights, independence, choice and inclusion*. Report, January 2004 www.dh.gov.uk/assetRoot/04/07/47/27/04074727.pdf

Lee, J.A.B. (2000) *The empowerment approach to social work practice: building the beloved community*. New York: Columbia Social Work Press.

Le Grand, J. and Estrin, S. (1990) *Market Socialism*. Oxford: Clarendon Press.

Levitas, R. (1986) *The ideaology of the new right*. Cambridge: Polity Press.

Letwin, O. (2004) Interview, *Today*, BBC Radio 4,2 Dec, 08:18.

Lewis J. (1999) The concepts of community care and primary care in the UK: the 1960s to the 1990s. *Health and Social Care in the Community*, **7**(5): 333–341.

Lewis, J. (2001) Reflections on evaluation in practice. *Evaluation* 7(3): 387–394.

Lewis, J. Bernstock, P. and Bovell, V. (1995) The community care changes: unresolved tensions in policy and issues in implementation, *Journal of Social Policy*, 24(1): 73–94.

Lewis, J. and Glennerster, H. (1996) *Implementing the new community care.* Buckingham: Open University Press.

Lewis, J. and Meredith, B. (1988) *Daughters who care*. London: Routledge.

Licht, S. (1968) *Rehabilitation medicine*. Baltimore: Waverly Press.

Lindsey, M. (2002) Comprehensive healthcare services for people with learning disability. *Advances in Psychiatric Treatment,* (8),138–148.

Lipschitz, D.S., Kaplan, M.L., Sorkenn, J.B., Faedda, G.L., Chorney, P. and Asnis, G. (1996) Prevalence and characteristics of physical and sexual abuse among psychiatric outpatients. *Psychiatric Services*, 47: 189–91.

Liss P. (1998) Assessing health care need: the conceptual foundation, in Baldwin S (ed) *Needs assessment and community care*. London: Butterworth Heinemann.

Lister, R. (1998) In from the margins: citizenship, inclusion and exclusion, in M. Barry and C. Hallett (eds.) *Social exclusion and social work*. Lyme Regis: Russell House Publishing.

Loney, M. (1986) *The politics of greed*. London: Pluto Press.

Longacre Inquiry (1998) *Independent Longacre inquiry*. Buckinghamshire: Buckinghamshire County Council.

Lord Chancellor's Department (1997) *Who decides? Making decisions on behalf of mentally incapacitated adults*. London: HMSO.

Lord Chancellor's Department (1999) *Making decisions, the government's proposals for making decisions on behalf of mentally incapacitated adults*. London: HMSO.

Lupton, C. (1992) Feminism. managerialism and performance management, in Langan, M. and Day, L. (1992) *Women, oppression and social work*. London: Routledge.

Lymbery, M. (1998) Care management and professional autonomy: the impact of community care legislation on social work with older people. *British Journal of Social Work,* 28(3): 863–878.

Lymbery, M. (2005) *Social work with older people: context policy and practice*. London: Sage Publications.

Lyon, J. (2005) A systems approach to Direct Payments: a response to friend or foe? Towards a critical assessment of Direct Payments. *Critical Social Policy,* 25 92: 240–252.

MacKenzie, F. (2005) The roots of biomedical diagnosis, chapter 3 in G. Grant , P. Goward , M. Richardsoon, and R. Ramcharan (eds) (2005) *Learning disability: A lifestyle approach to valuing people*. Buckingham: OU Press.

MacKenzie, S. (2004) Will he?, in *Guardian Weekend*, 25 Sep. (online).

Mandelstam, M. (1999) *Community care practice and the law*, 2nd edition. London: Jessica Kingsley Publications.

Mangen, S. (1985) *Mental health care in the European Community.* London: Croom Helm.

Mansell, J. and Beadle-Brown, J. (2005) Person centred planning and person centred action: a critical perspective chapter 2 in P. Cambridge, and S. Carnaby. (eds) (2005) *Person centred planning and care management with people with learning disabilities.* London: Jessica Kingsley.

Maria Colwell inquiry report (1974) *Committee of inquiry into the death of Maria Colwell.* East Sussex Social Services.

Martin, J.I. and Knox, J. (2000) Methodological and ethical issues in research on lesbians and gay men. *Social Work Research,* Vol. 24,1: 51–59.

Marwick, A. and Parrish, A. (2003) *Learning disabilities: themes and perspectives.* Edinburgh: Butterworth Heinemann.

Matthews, D. (2003) Action for health. *Learning Disability Practice,* 6 (5): 16–19.

Matthews, D. and Hegarthy, J. (1997). 'Ok' health check: health assessment checklist for people with learning disability. *British Journal of Learning Disabilities,* 25(4): 138–143.

Mayo, M. (1994) *Communities and caring. The mixed economy of welfare.* Basingstoke: Macmillan.

McCarthy, M. (1989) *The politics of welfare.* London: Macmillan.

McConkey, R. (2004) *Definition of learning disability* on Mexico Child link website. www.mexico-child-link.org/learning-disability-definition.htm

McCreadie, C. (2001) *Making connections: good practice in the prevention and management of elder abuse.* London: Kings College London.

McDonald, C and Harris, J. (2000) Post-Fordism, the welfare state and the personal social services: a comparison of Australia and Britain. *British Journal of Social Work,* 30(1): 51–70.

McMullen, K. (2003) *The direct approach: disabled people's experience of Direct Payments.* London: Scope.

Means, R. and Smith, R. (1998) *Community care: policy and practice*, 2nd edition. London: Macmillan.

Means, R., Richards, S. and Smith, R. (2003) *Community care policy and practice*, (3rd ed). Hampshire: Palgrave Macmillan.

Mencap (2004) *Treat me right! Better healthcare for people with a learning disability.* www.mencap.org.uk/download/treat_right.pdf

Mental Capacity Act (2005) Office of Public Sector Information via www.opsi.gov.uk/acts/acts2005/20050009.htm

Mental Health Act (1983) London: The Stationery Office.

Mesibov, G. (1990) Normalization and its relevance today. *Journal of Autism and Developmental Disorders*, 20(3): 379–91.

Messman-Moore, T.L. and Long, P.J. (2000) Child sexual abuse and revictimisation I: the form of adult sexual abuse, adult physical abuse and adult psychological maltreatment. *Journal of Interpersonal Violence*, **15**(5): 489–502.

Middleton, L. (1994) in Nolan, M. and Caldock, K. (1996, p80) Assessment: identifying the barriers to good practice. *Health and Social Care in the Community*, 4 (2) 77–79 Blackwell Science.

Milburn, A. (2002) Speech to Association of Directors of Social Services, 17 Oct. (online).

Milner, J. (2001) *Women and social work: Narrative Approaches*. Basingstoke: Palgrave.

Milner, J. and O'Byrne, P. (1998) *Assessment in social work*. London: Palgrave.

Minichiello, V. (2000) in Secker, J. et al. (2003, p253) Promoting independence: but promoting what and how? *Ageing and Society*, 23, 2003 375–391. Cambridge University Press.

Minois, G. (1989) *History of old age, from antiquity to the renaissance*. Chicago: The University of Chicago Press.

Mishra, R. (1984) *The welfare state in crisis*. New York: St Martins Press.

Moore, J. (2000) Adult protective services and older lesbians and gay men. *Clinical Gerontologists*, 21(2), 61–64.

Morgan, O. (1998) *Who cares? The great British health debate*. Abingdon: Radcliffe Medical Press.

Moss, S.C., Prosser, H., Ibbotson, B. and Goldberg, D.P. (1996) Respondent and informant accounts of psychiatric symptoms in a sample of patients with learning disability. *Journal of Intellectual Disability Research*, 40: 457–465.

Mount, B. and Zwernik, K. (1988) *It's never too early, it's never too late; a booklet about personal futures planning*. St Paul, MN: Metropolitan Council.

Mouzelis, N. (2001) Reflexive modernization and the Third Way: the impasses of Gidden's social democratic politics. *Sociological Review*: 436–456.

Munday, B. (1989) *The crisis in welfare*. London: Harvester Wheatsheaf.

Murray, J. and Adam, B. (2001) Aging, sexuality and HIV issues among older gay men. *The Canadian Journal of Human Sexuality*, Vol. 10 (3–4): 75–90.

Myers, F. (2004) *On the borderline? People with learning disabilities autistic spectrum disorders in secure, forensic specialist settings*. Scottish Development Centre for Mental Health. www.scotland.gov.uk/cru/resfinds/hcc39.pdf

Naidoo J, and Wills J. (1998) *Practising health promotion: dilemmas and challenges*. London: Baillière Tindall.

National Health Service and Community Care Act (1990) London: HMSO.

Nettleton, S. and Burrows, R. (1998) Individualisation processes and social policy, in Carter, J. (ed.) *Post-modernity and the fragmentation of welfare*. New York: Routledge.

NHS Scottish Executive (2004) *People with learning disability in Scotland: the health needs assessment report*. Glasgow: NHS Health Scotland.

Nibert, D., Cooper, S. and Crossmaker, M. (1989) Assaults against residents of a psychiatric institution: residents' history of abuse. *Journal of Interpersonal Violence*, **4**(3): 342–9.

Nirje, B. (1969) *The normalization principle and its human management implications*, in R. Kugel and W. Wolfensberger (eds) Changing Patterns in Residential Services for the mentally retarded in Washingtom D.C, USA, The President's Committee on Mental Retardation, pp.257–87.

Nolan C. (1999) *Under the eye of the clock: a memoir.* London: Phoenix.

Nolan, M. (1997) Health and social care, what the future holds for nursing. Keynote address of Nursing Older Persons European conference at Harrogate.

Nolan, M. (2000) in Hancock, S. (2003) *Nursing Standard* 17, 48, 45–51.

Nolan, M., Davies, S. and Grant, G. (2001) *Working with older people and their families: key issues in policy and practice.* Buckingham: Open University.

Northfield, J. (2003) *What is learning disability* on NHS National Electronic Library for Health (NeLH) http://libraries.nelh.nhs.uk/learningdisabilities/viewResource.asp?uri=http://libraries.nelh.nhs.uk/common/resources/?id=31736

Northway, R., Hutchinson C. and Kingdon A. (eds) (2005) *A vision for learning disability nursing: a discussion document.* The United Kingdom Learning Disability Consultant Nurse Network, July 2005, via The National Network Learning Disability Nurses www.nnldn.org.uk/

O'Brien, J. (1988) *Framework for Accomplishment.* Decatur, Georgia: Responsive Systems Associates.

O'Brien, J., Pearpoint, J. and Forest, M. (1993) PATH: *A workbook for planning positive futures.* Toronto: Inclusion Press.

Ogg, J. and Bennett, G.C.J. (1992) Elder abuse in Britain. *British Medical Journal*, 305: 998–999.

Oliver (1996) *Understanding disability: from theory to practice.* Basingstoke: Macmillan.

Oliver, M. (1990) *The politics of disablement.* Basingstoke: Macmillan,

Oliver, M. and Sapey, B. (1999) *Social work with disabled people* (2nd ed). Hampshire: Macmillan Press.

Orme J. (1998) Community care: gender issues. *British Journal of Social Work*, 28: 615–622.

Oswin, M (1978) *Children living in long-stay hospitals.* London: Heinemann.

Parker, G. (1985, 1990) *With due care and attention.* London: FPSC.

Parker, R. and Aggleton, P. (2003) HIV and AIDS-related stigma and discrimination: a conceptual framework and implications for action. *Social Science and Medicine*, 57: 13–24.

Parton, N. (ed.) (1996) *Social theory, social change and social work.* London: Routledge.

Pascal, G. (1986) *Social policy*. London: Allen and Unwin.

Paterson, B. (2001) Myth of empowerment in chronic illness. *Journal of Advance Nursing,* 34(5); 574–81 (in *Relationship centred care*, Nolan).

Paton, C. (1994) Planning and markets in the NHS, in Bartlett, W. et al. (eds) *Quasi-markets in the welfare state*. Bristol: SAUS.

Pearson, C. (2000) Money talks? Competing discourses in the implementation of direct Payments. *Critical Social Policy*, 2000, Volume 20(4). London: Sage Publications.

Pease, B. (2002) Rethinking empowerment: a postmodern reappraisal for emancipatory practice. *British Journal of Social Work*, Vol. 32, 135–147

Perez, W. (undated) *Top ten tips for effective consultation.* Learning about intellectual disabilities website (2005) St George's, University of London. www.intellectualdisability. info/values/top_ten_tips.htm

Perring, C. (1989) *Families caring for people diagnosed as mentally ill*. London: HMSO.

Phillips, J. (1996) in Parton, N. (ed) *Social theory, social work and social change*. London: Routledge.

Phillipson, C. (1989) in Thompson, N. (1993; p205) *Anti-discriminatory practice*. Macmillan.

Piachaud, J. and Rohde, J. (1998) Screening for breast cancer is necessary in patients with learning disability. *British Medical Journal*, 316, 1979.

Pillemer, K.A. and Moore, D.W. (1989) Abuse of patients in nursing homes: findings from a survey of staff *The Gerontologist*, 29(3), 314–20

Pillemer, K.A. and Moore, D.W. (1990) Highlights from a study of abuse in nursing homes. *Journal of Elder Abuse and Neglect*, **2**(1/2), 5–29

Plant, R. (1984) *Equality, markets and the state*. Fabian Society Pamphlet no 494.

Pollner, M. and Rosenfeld, D. (2000) The cross-culturing work of gay and lesbian elderly: *Advances in Life Course Research*, Vol. 5: 99–117.

Postle, K. (2002) Working 'between the idea and the reality': ambiguities and tensions in care managers' work, *British Journal of Social Work*, 32:335–351.

Powell, F. (2001) *The Politics of Social Work*. London: Sage.

Powell, M. (ed.) (2002) *Evaluating New Labour's welfare reforms*. Bristol: The Policy Press.

Priestley, M. (1999) *Disability politics and community care*. London: Jessica Kingsley Publishers.

Pritchard, J. (1990) Old and abused. *Social Work Today*, 15 February: 22.

Pritchard, J. (1992) *The abuse of elderly people : a handbook for professionals*. London: Jessica Kingsley.

Pritchard, J. (1993) *Gang Warfare. Community Care,* 8 July: 22–23.

Pritchard, J. (1995) *The abuse of older people*. London: Jessica Kingsley Publishers.

Pritchard, J. (1996) *Working with elder abuse*. London: Jessica Kingsley Publishers.

Pritchard, J. (1997) Vulnerable people taking risks – older people and residential care, in H. Kemshall and J. Pritchard (eds) *Good Practice in risk assessment and risk management 2 – protection, rights and responsibility*. London: Jessica Kingsley Publishers.

Pritchard, J. (1999) *Elder abuse work, best practice in Britain and Canada*. London: Jessica Kingsley Publishers.

Pritchard, J. (2001) *Male victims of elder abuse, their experiences and needs*. London: Jessica Kingsley Publishers.

Puri, B.K., Lekh, S.K., Langa, A., Zaman, R. and Singh, I. (1995). Mortality in a hospitalized mentally handicapped population: a 10-year survey. *Journal of Intellectual Disability Research*, 39: 442–446.

Quam, J.K. (1993) Gay and lesbian aging. Children, youth and family consortium SIECUS report June/July.

Quareshi, H. and Walker, A. (1989) *The caring relationship*. London: Macmillan.

Race, D. (ed) (2002) *Learning disability: a social approach*. London: Routledge.

Ramon, S. (1991) (ed.) *Beyond community care*. Basingstoke: Macmillan Education.

Redding, D. (1991) Exploding the myth. *Community Care*, 12.12.91.

Redfern, S.J. (1998) Long-term care: is there still a role for nursing? in Jack, R. (ed) *Residential v. community care*. Basingstoke: Macmillan.

Richards, S. (2000) Bridging the divide: elders and the assessment process. *British Journal of Social Work*, 30: 37–49.

Richardson, M. (2005) Critiques of segregation and eugenics, chapter 4 in G. Grant , P. Goward , M. Richardson, and R. Ramcharan (eds) (2005) *Learning disability*: *A lifestyle approach to valuing people*. Buckingham: OU Press.

Ricupero, R. (1998) Through a glass darkly. *The World Today*, 54(11): 277–278.

Robbins, D. (1990) *Voluntary organisations in the European Community*. Voluntas,1,2, p.103.

Robertson, J., Emerson, E., Gregory, N., Hatton, C., Kessisoglou, S. and Hallam, A. (2000b) Receipt of psychotropic medication by people with intellectual disability in residential settings. *Journal of Intellectual Disability Research*, 44: 666–676.

Robinson, R. and Le Grand, J. (eds.) (1994) *Evaluating the NHS reforms*. Newbury: King's Fund Institute.

Rojek, C. (1988) *Social work and received ideas*. London: Routledge.

Roy, A., Martin, D.M. and Wells, M.B. (1997). Health gain through screening – mental health: developing primary health care services for people with an intellectual disability (1). *Journal of Intellectual and Developmental Disability*, 22; 227–239.

Ryan, J. and Thomas, F. (1987) *The politics of mental handicap*. London: Free Association Books.

Savage, S.P. and Robins, L. (1990) *Public policy under Thatcher*. London: Macmillan.

Schindler R. (1999) Empowering the aged – a post-modern approach. *International Journal of Aging and Human Development*, 49(3): 165–177.

Secker, J., Hill, R., Villeneau, L. and Parkman, S. (2003) Promoting independence: but promoting what and how? *Ageing and Society* 23, 2003 375–391 Cambridge University Press.

Sharkey, P. (1989) Social networks and Social Service workers. *British Journal of Social Work*, 19.

Shipman, A. (1998) The pump that won't be primed. *The World Today,* 54(12): 314–316.

Simanowitz, S. (1995) *Violence, harassment, and discrimination against disabled people in Great Britain, an annual report for the European Disability Forum by Liberty.*

Sinclair, A. and Dickinson, E. (1998) *Effective practice in rehabilitation; the evidence of systematic reviews.* Kings Fund, London.

Skerrett, D. (2000) Social work — a shifting paradigm. *Journal of Social Work Practice*, Volume 14, No I.

Smale, G. et al. (1993) in Braye, S. and Preston Shoot, M. (1995, p116) *Empowering practice in social care.* Open University Press.

Smith, G. (1989) Review, *Journal of Social policy*, 18, 4.

Smith, J., Rochester, C. and Hedley, R. (1995) *An introduction to the voluntary sector.* London: Routledge.

Social Care Institute for Excellence (SCIE) (2006) *SCIE research briefing 2: access to primary care services for people with learning disabilities.* www.scie.org.uk/publications/briefings/briefing02/index.asp

Social Services Parliamentary Monitor (2004) *£4.5 million allocated to boost Direct Payments. www.cadmus.co.uk*

Social Trends (2004) Social trends 2004.

Spandler, H. (2004) Friend or foe? Towards a critical assessment of Direct Payments. *Critical Social Policy*, 2004, Volume 24(2), 1: 87–209, London: SAGE Publications.

SSI: Department of Health Social Services Inspectorate (1992) *Confronting elder abuse*, in SSI London Region Survey. London: HMSO.

Stainton, T. (2002) Taking rights structurally: disability, rights and social worker responses to direct payments. *British Journal of Social Work*, 2002, Volume 32, 75 1–763, Oxford University Press.

Stanley, N., Manthorpe, J. and Penhale, B. (eds.) (1999) *Institutional abuse, perspectives across the life course.* London: Routledge.

Steiner, A. (2001) Intermediate care: more than 'a nursing thing'. *Age and Ageing* 2001, 30:433–435. British Geriatrics Society.

Stevenson, J. (2003) in Crouch, D. (2003 p20) Intermediary care, how nurses fit in. *Nursing Times*, 5 August 2003 Volume 99 No31.

Stevenson, O. (1996) *Elder protection in the community, what can we learn from child protection?* London: Crown Copyright.

Straus, D. and Kastner, T.A. (1996). Comparative mortality of people with developmental disabilities in institutions and the community. *American Journal on Mental Retardation*, 101: 26–40.

Sumner, K. (2004) Who are the real experts? *Community Care*, 29 Jan: 32–34.

Swain, J., Finklestein, V., French S. and Oliver, M. (editors) (1993) *Disabling barriers - enabling environments.* London: Sage.

Swain, J., French, S., Barnes, C . and Thomas, C. (eds.) (2004) *Disabling barriers, enabling environments,* 2nd edition. London: Sage.

Swantz, M. (1996) A personal position paper on participatory research: personal quest for living knowledge, *Qualitative Inquiry*, March, 2(1): 120–137.

Tait T. and Genders, N. (2002) *Caring for people with learning disabilities.* London: Hodder Arnold.

Taylor and Dodd (2003) *Journal of Adult Protection.*

Taylor-Goodby, P., Dean, H., Munro, M. and Parker, G. (1999) Risk and the welfare state. *British Journal of Sociology*, 50:2.

Thomas, D. and Woods, H. (2003) *Working with people with learning disabilities: theory and practice.* London: Jessica Kingsley.

Thompson, N. (1993) *Anti-discriminatory practice.* Macmillan.

Thompson, N. (1997) *Anti-discriminatory practice.* (2nd ed.) Basingstoke: Macmillan.

Thompson, N. (1998) *Promoting equality.* London: Macmillan.

Thompson, N. (1998) Social work with adults, in R. Adams, L.Dominelli, and M. Payne (eds.) *Social work: themes, issues and critical debates.* Basingstoke: Palgrave.

Thompson, N. (1999) *Promotion equality.* London: Macmillian.

Thompson, N. (2001) *Anti-discriminatory practice.* (3rd ed.) Basingstoke: Palgrave Macmillan.

Thompson, N. (2003) *Promoting equality: challenging discrimination and oppression.* (2nd ed.), Basingstoke: Macmillan.

Thompson, N. and Thompson, S. (2001) Empowering older people: beyond the care model. *Journal of Social Work*, Vol. 1 (1): 61–76.

Tilbury, C. (2004) The influence of performance measurement in child welfare policy and practice. *British Journal of Social Work*, 34(2): 225–234.

Titmuss, R. (1968) *Commitment to welfare.* New York: Pantheon Books.

Titmuss, R.M., Oakley, A. and Ashton, J. (eds.) (1997) *The Gift Relationship: From Human Blood to Social Policy.* revised edition. London: LSE Books.

Titterton, M. (2005) *Risk and risk taking in health and social welfare.* Jessica Kingsley Press.

Tones, K. (2002) Health promotion health education and the public health, in R. Detels, J. McEwen, R. Beaglehole, and H. Tanaka (eds.) *Oxford textbook of public Health*, 829–863. Oxford: OUP Oxford.

Townsend P. (1973) *The social minority*. London; Allen Lane.

Tredgold, R. (1909) The feeble-minded; a social danger. *Eugenics Review,* 1: 97–104.

Tsui, M. (2004) *Social work supervision: contexts and concepts*. Sage Publication.

Turner, S. and Moss, S. (1996). The health needs of adults with learning disabilities and the health of the nation strategy. *Journal of Intellectual Disability Research,* 40, 438–450.

Twigg, J. (1989) Models of Carers. *JSP*, 18(1): 62–3.

Twigg, J. (1997) Deconstructing the Social Bath: help with bathing at home for older and disabled people. *Journal of Social Policy*, **26**(2): 211–232.

Twigg, J. and Atkin, K. (1994) in Nolan, M. and Caldock, K. (1996 p80) Assessment: identifying the barriers to good practice. *Health and Social Care in the Community*, 4(2) 77–85 Blackwell Science.

Twigg, J. et al. (1990) *Carers and services: a review of research*. London: HMSO.

Ungerson, C. (1987) *Policy is personal*. London: Tavistock.

Ungerson, C. (1990) *Gender and caring*. Hemel Hempstead: Harvester and Wheatsheaf.

Ungerson, C. (1997) Caring and citizenship: a complex relationship, in Bornat, J. et al. (eds.) *Community Care: A Reader (2nd ed)*, (1997), 144–152. Hampshire: Macmillan Press in association with The Open University.

Unity Sale, A. and Leason, K. (2004) Is help easily at hand? *Community Care Magazine*, 6–12 May 2004: 28–31.

Valuing People Support Team Newsletter May 2004 www.valuingpeople.gov.uk/documents/NewsletterMay2004.pdf

Wade, S. and Lees, L. (2002) The who, why, what of intermediate care. *Journal of Community Nursing,* October 2002 Volume 16; Issue 10.

Wahler, J. and Gabbay, S.G. (1999) Gay male aging: a review of the literature. *Journal of Gay and Lesbian Social Services*, Vol.6(3): 1–20.

Walker, A. (1982) *Community care.* Oxford: Blackwell and Robertson.

Walker, C. and Walker, A. (1998) Social policy and social work, in Adams, R., Dominelli, L. and Payne, M. (eds) *Social work: themes, issues and critical debates*. Basingstoke: Palgrave.

Walmsley, J. and Johnson, K. (2005) *Inclusive research with people with learning disabilities: past, present, futures*. London: Jessica Kingsley.

Warburton, N. (1994) *Philosophy : the basics,* (3rd ed). London: Routledge.

Ward, D. and Mullender, A. (1991) Empowerment and oppression: An indissoluble pairing for contemporary social work. *Critical Social Policy*, 11 (2): 21–9.

Wardhaugh, J. and Wilding, P. (1993) Towards an explanation of the corruption of care. *Critical Social Policy*, 37: 4–31.

Wells, M.B., Turner, S., Martin, D.M. and Roy, A. (1995). Health gain through screening – coronary heart disease and stroke: developing primary health care services for people with intellectual disability. *Journal of Intellectual and Developmental Disability*, 22: 251–263.

Wenger, G.C. (1990) in Jeffreys, M. (1990) *Growing old in twentieth century Britain*. London: Routledge.

Westbrook, M., Legge, V. and Pennary, M. (1993) Attitudes towards disabilities in a multi-cultural society. *Science and Medicine,* 36(5).

Whelan R. (1999) *Involuntary action? How voluntary is the voluntary sector?* London: Institute for Economic Affairs.

Whitford B. (2003) Taxing Times, *Guardian*, 20 June.

Wienhardt, L.S., Bickham, N.L. and Carey, M.P. (1999) Sexual coercion among women living with severe and persistent mental illness: review of the literature and recommendations for mental health providers. *Aggression and Violent Behaviour*, 4(3): 307–317.

Williams, C. (1995) *Invisible victims: crime and abuse against people with learning disabilities.* London: Jessica Kingsley Publishers.

Williams, F. (1992) in Biggs, 5 (1993, p153) User participation and interprofessional collaboration in community care. *Journal of Interprofessional*, Volume 7, No 2.

Wilmott, P. (1986) *Social networks, informal care and public policy*: London: Policy Studies Institute.

Wilmott, P. (1987) *Kinship in urban communities, past and present.* London: Policy Studies Institute.

Wilton, T. (1997) *Good for you: a handbook on lesbian health and wellbeing.* London: Cassell.

Winchester, R. (2004) Mental capacity. *Community Care Magazine*, 15–21 July 2004: 28–29.

Wolfenden Report (1978) *The future of voluntary organisations*. London: Croom Helm.

Wolfensberger (eds), *Changing patterns in residential services for the mentally retarded*, in Washington D.C., USA, The President's Committee On Mental Retardation: 257–87.

Wolfensberger, W. (1972) *The principle of normalisation in human services.* Toronto: National Institute of Mental Retardation.

Wolfensberger, W. (1983) Social role valorization. A proposed new term for the principle of normalization. *Mental Retardation,* 21: 234–239.

Wolfensberger, W. and Thomas, S. (1983) *Programme analysis of service systems: Implementing normalisation goals.* Downsview, Ontario: Canadian National Institute on Mental Retardation.

Wood Report (1929) Report of the mental deficiency committee cited in Atherton, H. (2003) *A history of learning disabilities*, chapter 3 in B. Gates (ed.) (2003) *learning disabilities* (4th ed.). Edinburgh:Churchill Livingstone.

World Health Organisation (1984). *Health promotion: a discussion document on the concept of and principles*. Geneva: WHO.

Wright, D. and Digby, A. (eds) (1996) *From idiocy to mental deficiency: historical perspectives on people with learning disabilities*. London: Routledge.

Young, I. (1990) *Justice and the Politics of Difference*. Princeton, NJ: Princeton University Press.

Index